The Story of Indian Archaeology 1784-1947

by
Sourindranath Roy

Published by

प्रत्नकीर्तिमपावृणु
The Director General
Archaeological Survey of India
New Delhi
2011

Published on the occasion of the celebration of 150 years of the Archaeological Survey of India

First printed in 1961
First reprint: 1996
Revised edition: 2011

Price: ₹ 90.00

Cover design by
Goodearth Publications, Eicher Goodearth Pvt Ltd, India

Printed at : India Offset Press, New Delhi.

Contents

Foreword
by Gautam Sengupta, Director General, ASI v

The Compiler's Apology
by Sourindranath Roy vii

The Setting of the Stage 1

The Antiquarian Prelude 12

From Antiquarian to Archaeology 23

Cunningham and the First Archaeological Survey 35

A Brief Setback and a Swift Recovery 41

Cunningham: The Second Phase 47

James Burgess 61

A Bleak Interlude 72

Curzon and the Dawn of a New Era 78

The Marshall Epoch 91

After John Marshall 114

Sourindranath Roy: Archivist and Historian
by George M Moraes 181

Foreword

This story of Indian archaeology was first published as an article by Sourindranath Roy in the ninth volume of *Ancient India*, the Archaeological Survey of India's journal of archaeological research. What began as an article of twenty-odd pages titled 'Indian Archaeology from Jones to Marshall' was later developed by Roy into a much more comprehensive history of Indian archaeology.

The Story of Indian Archaeology 1784-1947 was first published in 1961, as part of the celebrations of the ASI's centenary. The book was, in many ways, the first truly engaging and accessible account of the pioneering scholars, painstaking research and discoveries that defined archaeology in India from the time of the Orientalists to Indian Independence. Almost immediately upon its release, Roy's narrative acquired a seminal status – and few, if any, works on the history of Indian archaeology that have followed its publication can claim not to have derived inspiration from Roy's Story.

And yet, though fragments of his lucid prose survive in dozens of scholarly publications on archaeology, history has been less kind to Sourindranath Roy who was, unfortunately, forgotten.

In 2011, as the ASI celebrates its 150th anniversary, we hope to revive the memory of the brilliant scholar and fluid writer known to his friends as Sourin-*da* who, with the analytical command of his mind and the elegance of his pen, shed an illuminating light on the first two centuries of Indian archaeology.

Gautam Sengupta
Director General
Archaeological Survey of India

THE COMPILER'S APOLOGY

This small brochure on a great theme, the story of Indian archaeology, requires more than a formal word of apology. For, Indian archaeology with its long and eventful history and its magnificent record of achievements form the subject for anarrative of epical depth and dimensions, which will easily fill several ponderous volumes and will need, besides, a masterly pen to delineate it. That great narrative is beyond the scope of the present compilation, whose author, as it will readily become evident, has neither the scholarship nor the competence to attempt such a mighty task. What this compilation has tried to present is no more than a brief review of the leading trends which characterised the long march of Indian Archaeology from its antiquarian beginnings in the closing years of the eighteenth century to the culmination it reached in the late forties of the twentieth when, as a result of independence, it was able to achieve the right it had all along been struggling for not only to existence but to fullest self-realisation. The book has been projected to mark the Centenary of the first assumption by Government, in December 1861, of their moral responsibilities in respect to archaeological monuments in India, which are 'for variety, extent, completeness and beauty, unsurpassed, perhaps unequalled in the world'.

The period covered is long, and the materials regarding it are almost forbiddingly abundant. The problem which faces any narrator of its history is not of what to put in it but of what to leave out. I have, therefore, had to resort to a rigid selection and may be very rightly held guilty of giving some subjects a summary treatment and dealing with others at a great length. A personal bias in the case was almost unavoidable, but I have felt that an emphasis on what seemed to be of moment was perferable to a bare catalogue of dry dates and facts. It has not been possible for me, for instance, to deal except in a superficial manner, with archaeological developments in the ci-devant Indian States, for I had all the while to focus attention on the growth of the Archaeological Survey itself, whose Centenary, after all, we are celebrating now. There will be noticed other omissions dictated for the most part by the obvious limitations of space. I have, for instance, not been able even to touch the fascinating subject of the technical advances recently made not only in conservation and in treatment of decaying antiquities, but in the analysis and interpretation of archaeological finds. For these and other omissions I offer my unqualified apologies.

In compiling the brochure I have made extensive use of the official records of the Government of India, particularly those of the late Political, Public, Home and Public Works Departments, as well as the Department of Revenue and Agriculture, and it is my duty to express here my grateful thanks for the permission given me to utilise them. As to secondary sources I had to depend on a variety of published works, monographs and special antiquarian studies, books of travels and articles in periodicals, of which it is not possible to give here an exhaustive list. Specially deserving of mention, however, is the learned article by Sri A. Ghosh, Director General of Archaeology in India, on 'Fifty years of the Archaeological Survey of India', published in *Ancient India*

(Vol. 9, 1953). On this I have most liberally drawn. As the brochureis intended for the general reader I have avoided as far as possible burdening the text with references to the sources used.

Finally, it is necessary to add that the entire conception of the brochure owes its origin to Sri A. Ghosh. It was his idea to issue it on the occasion of the centenary of the historic organisation over which he presides now with distinction. He has helped me at every stage of the work sparing neither time nor trouble to give me the benefit of his advice and guidance and allowing me to draw, whenever necessary, on his unrivalled personal knowledge of the history of Indian archaeology. It is my pleasant duty to record my gratitude here. My thanks are also due to Sri M. Venkataramayya, Superintendent, Archaeological Survey of India, who has seen the work through the press and but for whose kind help it would not have seen light at all. I also take the opportunity of expressing my thanks to the Government of India Press, Faridabad, for bringing this brochure out at an almost incredibly short notice.

NEW DELHI, **Sourindranath Roy**
7 DECEMBER, 1961.

THE STORY OF INDIAN ARCHAEOLOGY

1784-1947

THE SETTING OF THE STAGE

ARCHAEOLOGY has come to acquire for modern India a significance which is at once deeper and subtler than a strict definition of the term as a scientific discipline would seem to imply. The reason, however, is not far to seek. For what archaeology has achieved for her, albeit unconsciously, is nothing short of a revolution, a revolution in her own conception of her history and personality. It has enabled her to establish her lost links with a great past whose magnificence was beyond her distant dreams. It has provided her with a vast and impressive background stretching back to the dimly lit dawn of prehistory and splendidly befitting her recently acquired greatness as a member of the comity of nations. Finally, by making her proudly conscious of a past replete with great achievements, it has made her also hopeful of a future worthy of that past. To put it briefly, it is archaeology which, more than anything else, has helped her to rediscover herself, to win back, so to say, her long-lost identity.

Archaeology is thus no outward frill, no ornamental embroidery on modern Indian history. It is something deeply rooted in the country's very existence, and constitutes almost a moral and spiritual necessity.

Yet the urge for archaeological investigations took a long time to germinate on the Indian soil. We hardly find any trace of it in the past history of the country. Ancient India never seems to have experienced it. Medieval India remained practically unaffected by it to the end.

To stress this is not to suggest even remotely that our forebears were devoid of any genuine feeling for the past. Yet, when all is said, the fact remains that they seldom evinced either any intellectual curiosity about its material vestiges or any scholarly inclination, to say nothing of competence, to understand their significance. An Asoka might feel anxiety, rare in his days, to conserve the sacred edifices enshrining the memory of departed saints. A Rudradaman might take justified pride in the renovation he had ordered of a historic dam falling into ruins. A Firuz Shah might set an example by according the highest priority to the repair of ancient monuments. But such acts, when they did not reflect a pious purpose or a statesmanlike intention, were usually prompted by aesthetic considerations. They had little to do with scholarly interests in mere historical evidence.

It is not in the least surprising that ancient India, unlike ancient Babylon, failed to throw up an antiquarian of the calibre of a Nabonidus, for a second Nabonidus is yet to be encountered in history. What is surprising is that in the whole of her literature, despite its unmistakable brilliance and almost frightening abundance, one cannot find a single author evincing a genuine antiquarian feeling, let alone impulse for prehistorical enquiries. It is true that the Vedic literature reflects an awareness, albeit extremely hazy, of the prehistoric times which witnessed the Indo-Aryan *Völkerwanderung* as also the encounter of the newcomers with the 'noseless' 'black-skinned' and 'phallus-worshipping' autocthons 'of alien speech', but the allusions to these events are too vague and too fragmentary to enable a correct assessment of the genuineness of the tradition. The Epics likewise speak of an earlier 'time without a ruler and full with terror' when people lived in promiscuity and utter lawlessness, devouring one another until they met together and chose themselves a king. The picture, however, hardly fits the more primitive conditions of the Indo-Aryans, and the narrators who told such tales were evidently influenced by popular theories of their own times. The Epics, moreover furnish other explanations of social evolution more undisguisedly mythical, and the later speculations on the subject seldom reflect a more rational or objective approach. They resulted in no ordered attempt to recover the material traces of past ages.

Conscious of living in a world which was part of an elaborate and self-complete religio-metaphysical system and which not only denied the reality both of time and space but rejected the very idea of change in the material sense of the word, the mind of the ancient failed to develop that empirical outlook, that concern for objective data which is the essential prerequisite of any scientific enquiry. It seldom looked back at the remote past, and when it did, it usually became entangled in a network of myths and pseudo-theorisings having no remote connexion with reality. No wonder that ancient Indian historiography never felt attracted to the mechanics either of cultural origins or of material changes affecting the ancient man. When it was not preoccupied with royal genealogies or successions of saints, mythical or real, it made its chief business to build up round historical events or characters romances conforming to the strict canons of Indian poetics.

The one historian in Indian antiquity to show a more objective approach was the Kashmirian Kalhana (11th century), a man of genius and considerable critical ability, who seems to have understood, however imperfectly, the value to historical reconstruction of the material remains of bygone ages. He not only attempted a thorough study of coins and inscriptions but made it a point personally to inspect ancient monuments and relics, and acquired in addition a thorough mastery of the topography of his land. All these means enabled him to compile a vast assemblage of factual data, which endowed his masterpiece, the *Rajatarangini*, an objectivity never before met with in Indian experience. Even so Kalhana was not entirely free from either mythological or pseudo-metaphysical influences. He showed little critical faculty when dealing with the periods for which he could not find any written record and allowed himself to be misled by legends and myths.

The advent of a new type of historiography under the aegis of Islam, about a century later, hardly effected any change in the situation, and the blank in Indian antiquarian thinking and efforts continued to remain as wide and as formidable as before. The new historiography showed a deeper concern for source-criticism, topographical accuracy and chronological precision, but practically none for the material vestiges of the great civilisation which it was obliged to encounter. Its chief weakness was its concentration on personalities, military happenings, and court cabals. The long range effect of social and economical forces, often deeply rooted in a past not readily recognisable, seldom attracted its attention. More immediately concerned as it was with the new order which Islam felt its mission to impose on the indigenous civilisation, Muslim historiography did not feel much interested in anything outside that order. But when it did, it usually turned for evidence to the extant legendary materials, involving itself, in consequence, in a maze of confused narratives in which fact and fiction were inextricably mixed up.

The one Muslim historian to show a true scientific understanding and an objective approach was Abu Raihan Al-Biruni. But the great Khwarizmian scholar preoccupied himself mostly with the literary antiquities of the Hindus and scarcely directed any attention to their material relics. Nor will it be correct to cite as a serious exception the example of Emperor Firuz Shah, whose interest in ancient Indian monuments did not extend beyond his chance encounter with the Asokan pillars at Topra and Meerut, and if, his own historian Shamsh-i-Siraz is to be believed, their subsequent removal to Delhi was prompted by the imperial desire to use them as trophies. Dramatic as this discovery was it did not create even a ripple in the soul of contemporary India. A more scholarly approach to objects surviving from the past was displayed, more than two centuries later, by the eminent historian Abul Fazl, whose masterly state-gazetteer, *Ain-i-Akbari*, embodies fairly accurate notices of a plethora of historical monuments and sites. Yet it is doubtful how far the historian himself comprehended the evidential value of the remains he wrote about. The great Abul Fazl, moreover, was an exception, and medieval India has nothing comparable to set beside his magnificent compilation.

If the Indo-Muslim historian failed to develop a true antiquarian spirit, the contemporary Hindu intellectual hardly proved his better. The advent of the Islamic Oikumenė had meant for him an almost complete break with his past. What fragmentary knowledge he used to have of it he had completely forgotten, and he had quietly replaced it by a fanciful reconstruction lavishly embellished with legends and myths. The climate was hardly favourable for the growth of any true spirit of intellectual enquiry, let alone a scientific curiosity about the past. What made possible the early flowering of the antiquarian impulse in Europe was the great Humanistic revival which had come immediately in the wake of the mighty Renaissance movement. But India did not experience any ferment remotely approaching that great European awakening. For the sprouting of a true antiquarian spirit on her soil what she primarily needed was the shock of an external stimulus. That stimulus ultimately came from the west, but only towards the end of the eighteenth century, when the ancien regime in India was already crumbling to pieces.

It was, however, no sensational find, comparable for instance to the Rosetta Stone or the Herculaneum papyrii, that first drew the mind of intellectual Europe to India's past. She was drawn to it by materials of quite a different order, to wit, the writings of a long succession of travellers who, since Marco Polo's days lured either by greed of gain or by simple curiosity, had actually visited this then little known land of wonder, and had afforded the west its first glimpse, albeit inadequate, of the grandeur that was her history. Among this motley crowd were not only eccentrics like Tom Coryat (1612-1617) who hiked all the way from Aleppo to Ajmer and did not leave a 'pillar or a tomb nor character unobserved in all Asia', but men endowed with solid ability and accurate power of observation like William Finch (1608-11) who had the distinction of being the first European to notice the Asoka pillars at Delhi and Allahabad and of leaving behind a journal which embodies one of the best accounts of the architectural wealth of Delhi, Agra, Lahore, Gwalior, Mandu and a host of other historical places.

There were others besides Finch who fell equally under the spell of India's fascinating monumental art. If the magnificence of Vijayanagara was described by Nicolo Conti (1419-44) and Athanasius Nikitin (1468), Ludovico di Varthema (1503-1508) and Duarte Barbosa, and the grandeur of Bijapur was portrayed by Ralph Fitch and Tavernier, the delineation of the marvels of Delhi and Agra devolved, among others, on Coryat, Withington, Tavernier and Bernier. Even the hidden wonders of the ancient rock-hewn temples did not escape the attention of these roving 'antiquarians'. The caves of Ellora were explored by Thevenot. Those at Kanheri were studied by Garcia da Orta and Dr. Gemelli Careri, while the famous cave of Elephanta found its delineators in Niebuhr, Dr. Fryer and Hamilton. One of the last in the line was the celebrated Joseph Tieffenthaler, who travelled extensively in India from 1743 and 1785 and left behind him a magnificient collection of plans and drawings (pl. XI) he had made of 'Cities, Forts, Temples, Idols' and 'other remarkable objects' in the vast sub-continent.

These early essays in antiquarian reconnaissance came steadily to be reinforced by enquiries of a different order which concerned themselves mainly with the literary remains of ancient India. Among the pioneers in the new field were : Abraham Rogers, whose *Open Door to Hidden Heathendom* (1651) was the first work to reveal to Europe the Brahminical doctrines and to make known, through translation, actual specimens of Sanskrit literature; Hanxlden (1699-1732), who compiled the first Sanskrit grammar in Latin; Calmette who in 1731 gave the west its first manuscript of the Rigveda and the Aitareya Brahmana; Father Pons, who in a letter dated 1740 furnished the first scholarly report on almost all aspects of Sanskrit literature. To these few names, chosen at random, should be added that of the Pondichery scholar Maridas Pillai, who materially helped the development of oriental scholarship by his French version of the Bhagavata Purana and other translations.

The impact of all these activities on the eighteenth century European scholarship, despite their obvious shortcomings, was as profound as it was compelling. They evoked the intellectual labours, for example, of historians like Joseph Duguigne, who was among the first to work out a plan of expanding the traditional scope of history by bringing within its limits the remotest parts of Asia, and to acquaint Europe not only with the nature and importance of the Buddhist religion but with its all-pervasive influence on Central Asia and China. But none was perhaps more profoundly stirred by these pioneer antiquarian efforts than Dr. Samuel Johnson and his friend and associate Sir William Jones (pl. I), two of the greatest minds which eighteenth century European enlightenment threw up. Though not an antiquarian himself, Johnson was the first not only to perceive the supreme need for systematic investigations being undertaken of India's past vestiges, but also to impress this need on the then Supreme Government in the country. How deeply he was exercised by the problem can be best read in the extracts, given below, from what he wrote on the subject to Governor-General Warren Hastings on 30 March 1774 :

> 'I can only wish for information, and hope that a mind comprehensive like yours will find leisure amidst the cares of your important station to enquire into many subjects, of which the European would either thinks not at all, or thinks with deficient intelligence and uncertain conjecture. I shall hope that he who once intended to increase the learning of his Country by the introduction of the Persian language, will examine nicely the tradition and histories of the East that he will survey the remains of its ancient Edifices, and trace the vestiges of its ruined cities; and that at his return we shall know the arts and the opinions of a race of men from whom very little has hitherto been derived.'

Such an appeal and from such a man could not have gone in vain, and it would be no wild conjecture to say that much of what Hastings did to revive Persian and Sanskrit studies in India was largely inspired by an impassioned voice calling out to him from thousands of miles away.

Yet no systematic plan was formulated to translate into reality the magnificient ideas which Dr. Johnson wanted to disseminate. That task had to wait till Sir William Jones, the other master mind who had caught the same fire, arrived in India as Puisne Judge of the Calcutta Supreme Court, and was able to take it up as the one great mission of his eventful life. A distinguished scholar and linguist who had already familiarised himself with some of the classics of India, Sir William brought to his task an exceptionally cultivated and informed mind and as a necessary first step towards its accomplishment he gathered round him a band of enthusiastic antiquarians with whose active collaboration he was able to form on 15 January 1784 under the name 'Asiatick Society' an institution for enquiring, among other things, 'into the History.........the Antiquities, Arts, Sciences and Literatures of Asia'.

Jones was by no means without any precursors in the field he had chosen, but the latter's interest in antiquities seldom stretched beyond the dilettantes' in the curious, the beautiful or the old. To Jones alone belongs the distinction of being the first to realise the need for co-ordinating antiquarian efforts of every variety that were being made in the country and also to find the means by which this coordination could be effected and further investigations conducted on systematic lines. Once started, the Society thrived rapidly and contributions commenced pouring in upon it from all quarters, announcing new finds or new interpretation of materials already known. A journal,

The Asiatick Researches, was started in 1788 to make known the results of these new efforts, and a museum was set up in 1814 to house the objects collected by the Society's growing band of workers. The start made in Bengal was soon followed up in other parts of India, and 'Literary Societies' modelled on the Asiatic Society made their appearance in Bombay and Madras. Thus the stage was finally set for an enthusiastic army of enquirers to pursue systematic investigations of Indian antiquities.

THE ANTIQUARIAN PRELUDE

THE scholars who under the learned guidance of Sir William Jones initiated antiquarian studies in the country may rightly be regarded as the true pioneers in the field of Indian archaeology. Yet it is doubtful if their activities were inspired by purely archaeological aims. Their immediate programme, ambitious as it was, envisaged a formidable multiplicity of topics for investigation including, for instance, geology and pure mathematics, ethnography and mechanics, geography and religion, mineralogy and politics, grammar and and rhetoric, music and agriculture, architecture and medicine. Archaeology could only have a very low priority in this extremely crowded programme.

Moreover, as could be expected, the pioneers had hardly any precise idea as to the correct scope of the archaeological science. Of the techniques of that science, whether relating to survey, or to excavation or interpretation they seemed to know almost next to nothing. Trained and disciplined in literary and linguistic investigations they naturally felt more attracted towards the literary remains of the past than its material vestiges. Even those, who like H.T. Colebrooke,could realize that 'in the scarcity of authentic materials for the ancient and even the modern history of the Hindu race' the importance 'attached to all genuine monuments was amply justified', firmly adhered to the conviction that the function of the monuments was simply to 'elucidate the scattered information which can yet be collected from the remains of Indian literature'.

It is, therefore, not in the least surprising that the activities of the pioneers were from the very start limited mostly to the translation and interpretation of ancient texts and epigraphs or to highly speculative dissertations. The worst example of this is provided by Francis Wilford's highly fanciful interpretations of the Ellora and Salsette inscriptions and his still more extravagant pseudo-antiquarian researches, published between 1792 and 1822, in which important historical information is found buried under a mass of immature conjectures. An event of great significance which, had it been followed up, might have led to important discoveries, took place a little before April 1786, when a Madras peasant found below the ruins of a Hindu temple near Nellore a collection of Roman coins and medals belonging to the second century A.D. But few, it appears, understood the real significance of the find. But this is not to say that the pioneers were totally indifferent to ancient relics and monuments. The glowing accounts which many of them have left behind of ancient architectural remains in particular would belie any such notion. But their interest in the remains seldom extended beyond a romantic appreciation of their compelling charm or overawing grandeur as magnificent artistic achievements, it scarcely took the shape of a scientific response to the challenge they represented as historical evidence. There were few measurements and no plans, and the illustrations were usually of little use for scholarly purpose.

Yet the debt which Indian archaeology owes to these early enthusiasts,—to these 'closet archaeologists', as Cunningham picturesquely calls them, seems to be immeasurable by any reasonable standard. The man to whom it was perhaps most indebted was Sir William Jones himself, who overshadowed all his contemporaries as much by the magnitude of his scholarship as by reason of the far-reaching significance of his discoveries. His brilliant discovery of the synchronism between Chandragupta Maurya (Sandrakottos of the Classical writers) with Alexander the Great provided Indian archaeology with its first positive date which, remained for many years to come 'the sole firm ground in the quick-sands of Indian history'. It has recently been claimed that the same synchronism had been proposed a few years earlier by the French historian Duguigne. That, however, does not detract from the value of Sir William's contribution. Neither he nor any of his contemporaries seems to have been aware of the French savant's findings and the distinction of making the synchronism known to the world of scholarship is due to Sir William alone.

Sir William was equally responsible for fixing the location of the classical Palibothra at the confluence of the Ganga and the Son, thus providing a starting point from which future investigation of ancient Indian geography could proceed. Equally far-reaching in its effect was the discovery he made of affinities, till then unsuspected, between Sanskrit and Persian on the one hand and Greek, Latin, Celtic and the German languages on the other, a discovery which stimulated comparative study of languages as a key to the early human past, and was to colour archaeological thinking in Europe and Asia throughout the nineteenth century.

Sir William's contributions in the field were richly supplemented by those of his close associate Charles Wilkins, the first Englishman to acquire a thorough mastery of the Sanskrit language. To him belongs the credit of unlocking the mystery of the Gupta as well as the *Kutila* script, and of laying thereby the foundation of epigraphical studies in India. The growth of these studies was materially helped by the labours of an Indian scholar, Radhacanta Sarman, who could, in Jones' view, challenge comparison with a Scaligar or even a Bentley in the matter of textual editing. But it was H.T. Colebrooke and H.H. Wilson, two of the most ardent followers of the Jonesian tradition, who were responsible for placing Indian epigraphy, for the first time, on a firm and sound footing. By undertaking the editing of a fairly large collection of inscriptions, Colebrooke made infinitely easy the task of all future researchers in the field, and the general essay he contributed to *The Asiatick Researches* (Vol. IX) on the topic will always remain a monument not only of his scholarship and critical insight but of his methodical treatment of epigraphical problems. Wilson, who, on Colebrooke's departure from India in 1815, literally caught his mantle, will be chiefly remembered by his great masterpiece, *Ariana Antiqua*, which stands as a living memorial to the painstaking researches he carried out on the antiquities of Afghanistan. But his earlier pioneering work in Sanskrit epigraphy, stimulating, as it did, further activities in the field, was hardly less valuable to archaeology.

The achievements which stand to the credit even of lesser luminaries of the period have an equal claim to recognition. To Lt. Colonel Antoine Polier belongs the distinction of communicating to the world of learning the first objective account of the famous pillar at Firuz Shah's fort in Delhi (published in *The Asiatick Researches*, Vol. I, 1788). Captain James Hoare was responsible for making the first satisfactory eye-copy of the Asokan inscriptions on the same pillar (pl. XIII) as also of those found on the pillar standing in the Allahabad fort. Hoare also took accurate measurements and prepared sectional drawings of the important monuments in both the forts, all being incorporated in his since famous 'Book of Drawings and Inscriptions.' (pl. XII). Extensive extracts from these were published by J.H. Harrington in *The Asiatick Researches* (Vol. VII) in 1801. Among the discoveries with which Harrington himself was associated may be mentioned the celebrated Nagarjuni caves near Bodh Gaya. Of more immediate significance was the chance discovery of two urns in a stupa at Sarnath, of which Jonathan Duncan was the first to publish a report. The report evoked the curiosity of Indian scholarship about a type of monuments, till then entirely unknown, which, thenceforth, was destined to prove one of the most important factors in opening up India's past through coins and inscriptions, sculptures and cult objects dug out of them.

Less exciting, though by no means less important, was Mountstuart Elphinstone's account of his encounter with the great stupa at Manikiyala, which was destined | to yield in the not too remote future some of the most important materials of Indo-Scythian history. Yet another event which opened up grea ossibilities for future research, was the almost dramatic discovery by Captain E. Fell, of the magnificent stupa at Sanchi. In the study of Islamic monuments Ensign James T. Blunt broke a new ground by taking the measurements of the Qutb Minar and publishing them in *The Asiatick Researches* (Vol. IV) in 1795. Copies of Muslim inscriptions on the monuments were afterwards, in 1822, furnished by Walter Ewer. In the field of Rajput antiquities the role of the path-finder was competently played by Captain (later Colonel) James Tod who subsequently won celebrity as the author of the *Annals and Antiquities of Rajasthan*.

The lead given by the Bengal antiquarians found eager followers in other parts of the country. In western India Sir Charles Warre Malet opened up in 1794 an entirely new line of research by directing attention to an early script, very similar to the Asokan, which he had discovered in the caves near Ellora. The first detailed account, with measurements and drawings, of the same caves was contributed by him in the same year (pl. XIV). He was followed by Salt, who, in 1806, prepared a detailed description of the Kanheri caves in Salsette, illustrated by drawings and copies of sculptures. The impressive architectural remains at Bijapur, 'the Palmyra of the Deccan', earlier described by Major Moor in 1794, and noticed in 1808 by Sir James Mackintosh, the founder of the Literary Society of Bombay, formed the theme of an elaborate paper contributed by Captain Sydenham in 1811. A more comprehensive study of the same subject was produced afterwards, in 1819, by Colonel Sykes, who, a year later, supplemented Malet's description of the Ellora caves by a more scholarly dissertation of his own. The cave of Elephanta evoked a paper from the pen of J. Goldingham in 1794, and in 1813 an exhaustive study, illustrated by plans and copies of sculptures, from the pen of William Erskine, better known for his translation of the 'Memoirs of Babar' (published in 1823). To Erskine also belongs the credit of publishing the first notice of the wonderful caves at Ajanta.

In South India the first antiquarian studies were undertaken by William Chambers, who visited the imposing ruins of Mahabalipuram in 1772, and again in 1776. He described them in *The Asiatick Researches* in 1788. A more elaborate treatment of the subject was attempted by J. Goldingham in the same journal six years later. But the guiding spirit of antiquarian research in the south was Colonel Colin Mackenzie (1753-1821), who made it the principal aim of his life to penetrate 'beyond the common surface of the Antiquities' in order to recover 'the History and the Institutions of the South of India'. Although his multifarious duties, first as an officer of local Survey and since 1815 as the Surveyor-General of India, made continual calls on his time, talent and energy yet he was able to devote the best part of the thirty-eight years he spent in India to the exploration of historical sites and collection of antiquarian objects. He visited nearly every place of interest in peninsular India preparing in the course 2630 measured drawings and 78 plans all laid to scale. He also got together 6218 coins, 106 images and no less than 8076 inscriptions, providing thereby the basis for future researches on South Indian history and epigraphy. To Mackenzie also belongs the distinction of preparing th first careful plans and drawings of the great Buddhist stupa at Amaravati, which are still unsurpassed for accuracy as well as beauty of finish. It was he again who first called attention to the importance of the megalithic monuments of south India, thus opening up an entirely new field of investigation. Fate did not spare him either to complete his researches or to publish their results, but although not a writer himself, the splendid collection of antiquities he left behind him inspired writing in others.

About the same time as Mackenzie commenced his series of measurements and drawings a British water-colourist, Thomas Daniell, attacked the problem of architectural illustration from a somewhat different angle. Daniell started on a much larger canvas, executing water colours of a representative selection of monuments and edifices in all parts of India. His labours were given to the world in 6 large folio volumes embodying 120 coloured views, all engraved between 1790 and 1809. Daniell brought to his task a true painterly vision controlled by perfect draughtsmanlike skill, and even today his portrayals of Indian architecture bear the test of comparison with most successful photographs.

But all these were the results of individual efforts to which the Government of India seemed little inclined to lend its support. Even Mackenzie, whose contributions secured the approbation of the Court of Directors in London, was obliged to meet the expenses of his researches from his own slender purse. It is true in 1797 the Director called on all Presidencies to instruct government servants 'to transmit such information on the Chronology, Geography, ...the Arts and Sciences' of the country as the latter 'may be able to collect'; but nothing material came out of this spasmodic venture. A change in the situation was however presaged in 1800, when Francis Buchanan (later Buchanan Hamilton) was entrusted by Marquis of Wellesley to carry out a survey of the entire Mysore territory. Though primarily devoted to topographical and statistical matter the complete report embodied also interesting notices of the antiquities of the country, the first in practice to be published under official aegis.

In 1807 Government instituted a further survey embracing 'the whole of the territories subject to the immediate authority of the Presidency of Fort William as well as the adjacent Countries' and covering, among other matters, topography, history and antiquities, and on Buchanan devolved again the duty of executing it. For eight years he pursued his investigations in the districts of Dinajpur, Rangpur, Purnea, Bhagalpur, Bihar, Shahabad, and Gorakhpur, when his labours were brought to an abrupt close. The reports of these surveys, which for the most part remained unpublished, covered no less than thirty-seven volumes in addition to four volumes embodying over five hundred architectural and sculptural drawings and copies of sixty-two inscriptions, quite a large number of which were from Bodh Gaya.

It is not easy to form an idea of the great quality of Buchanan's work from Montgomerie Martin's eviscerated edition of his manuscripts. Martin's illustrations are generally poor representations of the originals. It is important to remember this because

Buchanan was one of the very few among his contemporaries to realise the value of detailed plans and exact measurements of ancient buildings and historical sites. His archaeological reconnaissances in eastern India were remarkable alike for sound judgement and conscientious accuracy, and when Cunningham, many years later, visited the places described by Buchanan he was struck by the thoroughness and the meticulous care with which the latter's work had been done.

No effort was made for many years to come to find a successor to Buchanan, who could carry on the work so splendidly started by the latter, and if the Government were apathetic to the need for a systematic exploration of archaeological sites they remained equally unconscious of their moral obligation to protect and conserve historical monuments. Sporadic endeavours were no doubt made from time to time to spare a little of public money for the fitful repair of one architectural piece or another. For instance, Lord Minto appointed a Committee to look after the maintenance of the Taj, and Moira ordered conservation work at Sikandra, Fatehpur Sikri and Rambagh, while under Lord Amherst elaborate repairs were undertaken of the Qutb Minar by Captain Robert Smith. But by themselves these measures meant little, and of a well-articulated plan to conserve ancient monuments there was hardly yet any sign. Even when financial assistance flowed to any work, it literally came in driblets. The sum made available for the maintenance of Rambagh, for instance, amounted to rupees ninety-three only, while the annual outlay on the conservation of the Taj and the tomb at

Sikandra taken together did not exceed a bare sum of one thousand rupees.

This apathy in the matter of conservation was matched by a similar indifference to acts of vandalism perpetrated on monuments. It was quite a common practice to demolish ancient edifices to make room for military barracks or to cart away the fragments of decaying monuments for ordinary building purposes. Even responsible officials and high dignitaries of state were not always above committing such acts. Under Moira steps were taken to dismantle the marble bath in Shah Jahan's palace for a gift to King George IV. This was later sold by public auction under Lord Bentinck's orders. During the latter's administration a move was made to demolish the Taj for the value of its marbles and also to lease the gardens at Sikandra to the Executive Engineer at Agra for speculative cultivation. Even a genuine antiquarian like Mackenzie did not find anything wrong in rifling the stupa at Amaravati of some of its finest sculptural components or in shipping them away to England. No doubt both the Bengal Regulation XIX of 1810 and its Madras counterpart (Regulation VII of 1817/817) invested the executive with power to intervene whenever any public edifice was exposed to the risk of misuse by private individuals. But this power did not extend to monuments in private ownership. The law moreover was helpless when a state official ordered the dismantlement of an ancient edifice or a Governor General himself engaged in gross acts of vandalism.

FROM ANTIQUARIANISM TO ARCHAEOLOGY

THE half-century following the formation of the Asiatic Society witnessed the germination of archaeological thinking from the seeds of antiquarian speculations. If the process was unusually slow the reason is to be sought not so much in public apathy to the systematic investigation of the past, which, as we have seen, was all through in evidence, but in the fact that archaeology, since its very inception, had been completely under the tutelage of the older discipline. Under the circumstances all enquiries into the bygone ages in India tended to degenerate into mere speculative endeavours drawing their inspiration either from linguistic researches or amateurish and unmethodical analysis of antiquarian odds and ends.

The man whose genius and labours helped archaeology to free itself from its antiquarian and literary affiliations was James Prinsep (pl. II), Assay Master, Calcutta Mint, from 1832 to 1840, who on his appointment as the Secretary of the Asiatic Society assumed the virtual direction of the entire field of archaeological work in India. By training and inclination Prinsep was essentially a man of science, and he brought to his task a scientific love of orderliness and precision and the scientist's mastery of factual details, which enabled him to march from discovery to discovery with a swiftness that still appears amazing. His acute reasoning power and unflagging industry was backed by an enthusiastic love of research, and he added to rare gifts of intellect, an amiable and generous disposition, giving all credit to his fellow-labourers and reserving none for himself, so that men worked as much to please him as for their own love of archaeological investigations. He was, in consequence, able to harness together all isolated efforts in the field and to transform the pursuit of India's past into one long voyage under his sole command.

An erudite scholar with a rich imagination and clear-sighted vision, a master in epigraphic and numismatic techniques in which he was without any rival, Prinsep was equally at ease in field-survey and precise recording, a predilection for which he had demonstrated as early as 1825 by executing a series of accurate plans and drawings of the streets and buildings of Banaras (pls. XV and XVI). His greatest contribution to archaeology consisted in the transformation he was able to effect of its entire character by directing it to systematic survey operations in the field. His public duties as Assay Master, combined with his epigraphical preoccupations, left him very little time to conduct such operations personally, but he encouraged others to undertake similar operations and took initiative in interpreting and publishing their results, as soon as they came to be known. He was among the first to visualise the great significance of the excavations carried out by Generals Ventura and Court in the Manikiyala Stupa in 1830, and in similar remains in the Indus-Jhelum region in 1833 and 1834, which brought to light not only huge hoards of Buddhist relics and sculptures but also coins and inscriptions revealing the existence of a new family of rulers, the Kushans.

Prinsep equally took the initiative not only in making known but in subjecting to an interpretative analysis the existing discoveries which W. Masson made in the course of his exploration of the ancient stupas in Afghanistan, particularly at the historical site of Begram, which brought to light for the first time the names of a considerable number of Graeco-Bactrian and Indo-Scythian dynasts of whom history had absolutely no knowledge, thus opening up an entirely new avenue for research. But these were not the only explorations whose results Prinsep felt it to be his duty to analyse and interpret. There were many more which he was himself responsible for inspiring and which received from him the same scientific treatment. Particular mention may be made here of the investigations carried out in Orissa by his close coadjutor Markham Kittoe which led to the discovery, among others, of the famous rock edicts of Asoka at Dhauli. But perhaps of greater importance were the operations which Alexander Cunningham undertook at the Dhamek stupa at Sarnath in 1834-35 and at the complex of ruins surrounding it in 1835-36 (pl. XXI), as they presaged the pattern which future archaeological explorations were to follow for many years to come. Cunningham's opening of the stupa at Sarnath was the first excavation of an ancient site to have been attempted in India as part of archaeological investigation; it succeeded in laying bare the complete structural history of a representative specimen of a most important class of historical monuments.

By focussing attention on the results of these as well as other explorations which followed in quick succession, Prinsep amply demonstrated what could be achieved by the continuation of laborious investigations in the field with patient research in the closet. Facts now began to pour in rapidly but Prinsep found no difficulty in ensuring that they were properly utilised. Since 1829 he had at his disposal a journal (known at first as *Gleanings in Science*, but rechristened in 1832 as *The Journal of Asiatic Society*), and this now became in his hands an efficient instrument both for coordinating and disseminating the results of all those investigations which he had himself planned or inspired. Prinsep eqally directed his attention to the conservation of the antiquities which had in ever-increasing numbers commenced collecting round him. He argued vehemently with Government the case for a national museum (pl. XIX), and the grant which he obtained in consequence enabled him to remould the embryonic museum of the Asiatic Society to his requirement and to develop it into a satisfactory repository for important archaeological finds.

But great as Prinsep was as an organiser, he was still greater as a discoverer, and Indian archaeology never produced another scholar who was responsible for as many discoveries made in as short a time. Most remarkable among Prinsep's achievements was the unlocking between 1834 and 1837, i.e., within the incredibly brief space of three years, the mystery of both the Kharoshthi and the Brahmi scripts, the effect of which was instantly to remove the thick crust of oblivion which for many centuries had concealed the character and the language of the earliest Indian epigraphs. Prinsep was led to the first discovery by the clue furnished to him by Masson who had independently found out the Greek equivalents of several royal names engraved in Kharoshthi on Indo-Greek coins. But the credit of minutely analysing the entire alphabet and of determining the value of the greater number of its component symbols belongs to Prinsep and to Prinsep alone.

Prinsep showed even greater ingenuity in deciphering the other ancient script, the clue to which he first obtained when, in June 1837, he received copies, made for him of the short epigraphs occurring on the pillars round the stupa at Sanchi. Each of these epigraphs ended with the same two letters, and it occurred to Prinsep, almost by inspiration, that the letters stood for the Indo-Aryan word *danam* (gift). Pursuing his investigation on this basis, Prinsep, at last, to quote his own words, 'became possessed of the whole alphabet, which I tested by applying it to the inscription on the Delhi column'. The decipherment of the records of Piyadasi incised on this column, as well as on others, which led to the identification of that monarch with Emperor Asoka, proved to be only the commencement of a series of exciting discoveries, in some respects even more important, for most of which again Prinsep himself was responsible. He crowned all these discoveries by identifying in 1838 the names of three Hellenistic Kings, Antiochus II, Ptolemy Philadelphos, and Magas of Cyrene in the Asokan inscription found on the Girnar rock (pls. XVII, XVIII and XX). This identification led to the establishment of the contemporaneity of the author of these inscriptions with those rulers and helped to place Indian archaeology for the first time on a secure chronological basis.

The programme of interpretative and analytical researches for which Prinsep made himself responsible could be successfully pursued because they were vigorously reinforced by careful exploratory operations in the field. Yet it is doubtful if either Prinsep or any of his colleagues understood the correct function of field-work, which was with them, as with many of their successors, a mere means to obtain plans of old buildings, new art-treasures, coins and epigraphic records. The main object of these early explorers was to discover the objects which would grace a museum rather than to procure the evidence which would lay bare a civilisation. In this respect the Indian archaeologist of the period was no better inspired than his colleagues in the Near East, who would rifle a Mesopotamian *tell* to find Assyrian sculptures or an Egyptian tomb to discover papyrii.

In the very midst of his brilliant discoveries Prinsep suddenly died on 22 April 1840 leaving Indian archaeology practically without a leader. He was at that time at the height of his abilities and yet just in the very prime of life. Though the impulse given by him was not lost, archaeological efforts which under his enlightened guidance had been consolidated into a single unified enterprise tended again to degenerate into isolated ventures moving erratically in diverse directions. Of his immediate successors the most prominent were Alexander Cunningham, Markham Kittoe, and Edward Thomas in North India, Sir Walter Elliott in south India, Dr. J. Stevenson, and Dr. Bhau Daji in western India each following his own line of work without any attempt at coordination.

Cunningham took up the investigation on the Indo-Greek and Indo-Scythic dynasties at the point at which Prinsep had left it and contributed much useful information that was unknown before him. He was also responsible for identifying the site of the ancient town of Sankisa and for minutely examining the stupas at Bhilsa. In the latter task he had the collaboration of Lieutenant F. Maisey. On Markham Kittoe devolved the task of preparing a minute survey of the viharas and the chaityas in Gaya and other places in Bihar. The result was a large collection of carefully executed drawings of select specimens of sculptures found by him at various sites. Kittoe also continued the excavations initiated by Cunningham in 1835-36 in the ruins at Sarnath, and was able in the course to determine the layout of the Buddhist monastery adjoining the Dhamek stupa (pl. XXII). Edward Thomas made Indian numismatics his special field of investigation and his numerous essays on the subject, embracing the long period of eighteen hundred years, from the third century B. C. to about the sixteenth century A.D., testify to the unusual range of his scholarship and technical competence. But he deserves to be remembered equally for the extensive excavations he carried out at Sarnath in continuation of Kittoe's earlier work there, and his report leaves little room for doubt that he had a very acute power of observation.

Elliott endeavoured to complete what Mackenzie had begun in the realm of epigraphy. He obtained copies of no less than five hundred and ninety-five inscriptions collected from Dharwar, Sonda and north Mysore. He also illustrated the history of the Chalukyas and other southern dynasties with the help of their coins, which he was the first to arrange systematically. Like him both Stevenson and Bhau Daji interested themselves primarily in epigraphy. To the former belongs the distinction of preparing the first reliable translation of the important cave inscriptions in western India. He also made substantial contributions in the deciphering of numerical figures in old inscriptions. Bhau Daji's title to fame rests, among other works, on his translation of the Ajanta epigraphs and also of the records of Rudradaman and Skandagupta on the Junagadh rock. It may be said without any deviation from the truth that he well upheld the cause of epigraphy in western India and the Deccan after Dr. Stevenson had passed away.

But two names which boldly stand out among the investigators of the post-Prinsep period are those of James Fergusson and Colonel Meadows Taylor (pl. III), because of the special significance of the investigations with which they were associated. Fergusson specialised in architectural surveys and between 1829 and 1847 made an extensive examination of the different types of ancient buildings. The results of these activities were embodied in two significant volumes *Illustrations of Rock-cut Temples of India* (London, 1845) and *Picturesque Illustrations of Ancient Architecture in Hindustan* (London, 1874) to be followed by his monumental *Handbook of Architecture* (London, 1855) the first illustrated history of Indian buildings and monuments. He also evolved a system of classification of buildings which, for many years to come remained the only tool for architectural surveys with his successors in the field.

Meadows Taylor was among the first to devote special attention to the megalithic tombs, many examples of which he discovered particularly in Shorapur in the Deccan, above the junction of the Bhima and the Krishna rivers. He opened a number of these tombs and compiled an accurate description of their structure and contents, and the three papers he published on the subject in the *Journal of the Bombay Branch of the Royal Asiatic Society* (III 1851, 179–93; and IV 1852, 380–429); and the *Transactions of the Royal Irish Academy* (XXIV, pt. III, 1865) testify to his having developed a technique of excavation far in advance of his time. Among Indian archaeologists he was, on all evidence, the first to grasp the true function of excavation and was also the first who actually drew and described sections with strata clearly distinguished and marked out (pls. XXIII and XXIV). He left behind no followers to continue his work and the technical methods he had evolved, excellent as they were, failed to survive him.

Taylor's achievements excepted, the period following Prinsep's death hardly made any constructive contribution to the development of the archaeological technique. Yet the period was fruitful in a most significant way. It witnessed the first deliberate attempt made by the State to take an active interest in Indian monuments. The decisive step was taken in this direction in May 1844, when, following a suggestion from the Royal Asiatic Society of the United Kingdom, the Court of Directors suggested to the Government of India 'the employment of some of our talented Officers' or 'any of the good means for getting copies of paintings not only in Ajanta but in other Caves and to preserve the Caves from dilapidation. At the same time they requested to be supplied with a series of drawings 'of objects of interest..... illustrative of the....phases, characters and conditions of its various tribes and peoples comprising architecture, implements costumes' etc., The Indian Government responded to the request by sanctioning a small sum for repairs to monuments like the cave temples of Ajanta and Ellora, while the Bombay Government mapped out a thirty-two year scheme for getting prepared the drawings of the principal objects of western India. The latter move was considered by the Court to be impractical. They, therefore, drew up a detailed plan for the early formation of a commission for collecting accurate, minute, and well-classified information as to the nature, the extent and the state of the existing monuments.

The plan underwent substantial modifications in the hands of Lord Hardinge, who suggested that the proposed Commission should be appointed 'till one or more Officers possessing habits of research and knowledge of Indian antiquities' had compiled preliminary reports upon each temple and building in detail, and mentioned Kittoe, Cunningham and Dr. Bird as the men who could be entrusted with the task. His view was that well-known antiquarians in Europe like Dr. H. H. Wilson, Eugene Burnouf, and Christian Lassen should prepare, on the basis of these reports, a set of queries the answer to which were to be found by their Indian colleagues by means of a detailed survey of all important monuments and sites. It was only at this stage that in Hardinge's view an Antiquarian Commission should be set up for selecting specimens of buildings worthy of delineation. This revised plan was approved by the Court and Kittoe was appointed to conduct operations in Bihar and Banaras. The only other results of this decision were the appointment of Major F. Maisey to draw the antiquities at Kalinjar and the sculptures at Sanchi, and of Captain Gill to copy the paintings in Ajanta and the Ghat caves, and the setting up of the Bombay Cave Temple Commission on whose recommendation Lt. Brett was commissioned in 1851 to take impressions of cave inscriptions.

These measures almost synchronised with an event of great importance, viz., the formation in 1847 of the Archaeological Society of Delhi, the first voluntary organisation to devote itself exclusively to archaeological work. The object of the new organisation, as defined by itself, was 'the investigation by means of plans, drawings, and elevations by inscriptional and........historical researches....of the ancient remains both Hindu and Mahomedan, in and around Delhi; and the institution of similar researches, in other parts of North Western Provinces'. As to its general approach, the Society announced that it considered it desirable 'to compare the remains of former ages, in various districts of the Country with those in existence in our immediate neighbourhood, so as to fix, beyond a doubt, the age of each by the style of the other'. The announcement remained no more than an idea. The Society was too short-lived to work it out. Yet as the first clear enunciation of the usefulness of stylistic evidence in solving problems in chronology it has an important place in the annals of Indian archaeology.

Happenings like these by themselves probably did not mean much. Yet they point unmistakably to the general awakening that was rapidly taking place in respect to the archaeological problems of the country. Signs could already be seen of a growing consciousness of the value of ancient relics and monuments and an increasing anxiety to explore and interpret them. There was equally in evidence not only a better understanding of archaeologlcal facts but a firmer grasp of their ımplications. To all seeming, archaeology had at last passed the stage of its childhood and was getting ready for the next stage in its career.

CUNNINGHAM AND THE FIRST ARCHAEOLOGICAL SURVEY

THE last two decades of the nineteenth century, as we have already seen, experienced an intellectual ferment in the course of which new aims and aspirations, albeit yet vague and indistinct, were forcing themselves into the understanding of Indian Archaeologists. The man on whom devolved the task of giving form and precision to this awakening was Alexander Cunningham (pl. IV), perhaps the greatest name associated with Indian archaeology during the century. Cunningham was among the first to realise the necessity for organising a country-wide survey of archaeological remains, and had as early as 1848 pleaded, without success, the case for such a survey in an article published in the Asiatic Society's journal under the caption 'Proposed Archaeological Investigations'. Initial failure did not, however, damp his courage. He stuck to his guns and continued agitating. The opportunity he was looking for came to him at last in November 1861, when he was able to place before Lord Canning an elaborate memorandum (pls. XXV and XXVI) emphasising the desirability of systematic and complete investigation into the country's archaeological resources. 'During the one hundred years of British Dominion in India', Cunningham argued 'the Government has done little or nothing towards the preservation of its ancient monuments, which, in the almost total absence of any written history, form the only reliable sources of information as to the early condition of the country'. He pointed out that many of these monuments were 'daily suffering from the effects of time', and that 'they would soon disappear altogether unless preserved by the accurate and faithful descriptions of the archaeologist', and concluded by saying that 'it would redound....to the honour of the British Government to institute a careful and systematic investigation of all the existing monuments of ancient India'.

Cunningham's arguments had a compelling effect and Canning felt convinced that 'it will not be to our credit, as an enlightened ruling power, if we continue to allow such fields of investigations, as the remains of the old Buddhist Capital in Behar, the vast ruins of Kanouj, the plains of Delhi, studded with ruins more thickly than even the Campagna of Rome, and many others, to remain without more examination than they have hitherto received'. He noted with regret that 'everything that has hitherto been done....has been done by private persons, imperfectly and without system', and could not resist feeling that 'there are European Governments which, if they had held our rule in India, would not have allowed this to be said'. The Governor General, therefore, decided to sanction a scheme of survey in northern India, the aims of which were defined to be 'an accurate description' illustrated by plans, measurements and drawings or photographs and by copies of inscriptions of such remains as deserve notice, with the history of them so far as it may be traceable, and a record of the traditions that are retained regarding them'. He also proposed that 'the work be entrusted to Colonel Cunningham', 'who has, more than any other Officer on this side of India, made the antiquities of the Country his study' (pls. XXVII and XXVIII). It was decided to give him a salary of Rs. 450 per month together with a field allowance of Rs. 250 and, what is more interesting, a share in the antiquities to be discovered by him.

The scheme accepted by Canning's Government was thus strictly limited to the survey and description of monuments. The question of their conservation was deliberately left outside it, as the Government had no desire to commit themselves to any future or unseen expenses. It was in their view a task which 'would require an expenditure of labour and money far greater than any Government of India could reasonably bestow upon it'. It would however be wrong to think that the Government minimised the importance of the task, for two years later they took the significant step of passing an Act (X) which invested them with the authority to 'prevent injury to and preserve buildings remarkable for their antiquity or for their historical and architectural value'. This augured a pronounced departure from the old policy of apathy and downright neglect and marked the opening of a new era in the history of Indian archaeology.

The conduct of the operations decided on by the Government was formally entrusted to Cunningham on the 1st December 1861 (pl. XXIX). The new Archaeological Surveyor brought to his task the ideas and the techniques he had inherited from the Prinsep age and a mind which was at that time essentially preoccupied with topographical problems, particularly those brought to the forefront by the recently published records of Fa-Hien and Hiuen-Tsang. No wonder, therefore, we find him dominated for the most part by the single idea of locating the holy places the Chinese pilgrims had traversed. 'In describing the ancient geography of India', Cunningham announced, 'the Elder Pliny, for the sake of clearness follows the footsteps of Alexander the Great. For a similar reason I would follow the footsteps of the Chinese pilgrim Hwen-Thsang, who, in the seventh century of our era, traversed India from west to east and back again for the purpose of visiting all the famous sites of Buddhist history and tradition' (pl. XXX).

During his first season Cunningham limited his activities to Bihar and Banaras identifying no less than twenty-four ruins in Bodh Gaya and elsewhere including the caves in the Barabar hills, excavated by Asoka. His tour was extended in the next season (1862-68) through Fatehgarh, Kanauj, Roorki, Kalsi, and Mathura to Delhi. He examined the ruins of Sankisa and, at Kalsi, made an impression of the famous rock inscription of Asoka identifying for the first time the name of Alexander of Epirus to whom the record made a reference. The next year the surveyor explored the ruins in Panjab and beyond, and worked at the identification of the cities and people described in the expedition of Alexander the Great. In his report of the season he described, among others, the ruins at Jamalgarhi and Yusufzai (pl. XXXI) and gave a detailed account of Taxila, Manikiyala, Sirhind and Thaneswar. The survey operations of the next season were devoted to the region between the Jumna and the Narmada. Thus by 1865 Cunningham had succeeded in covering the vast area stretching from Gaya in the east to the Indus in the north-west, and from Kalsi in the north to the Dhamnar caves in the south, having carefully surveyed and reported on every monument of note in all the historical sites visited by him.

Brilliant as these activities were, they were exclusively directed to the investigation of historical sites and monuments. Neither Cunningham nor any of his colleagues or associates devoted much thought to the problem of the pre-historic period in India. This blank in their efforts were however, more than adequately filled by the endeavours, not of any professional archaeologist, but of men working in fields altogether different. In January 1860 H.P.Le Mesurier of East India Railway sprung a surprise on the world of learning by discovering a large number of neoliths in the valley of the Tosney river. This was followed by a still greater surprise when Robert Bruce Foote of the Geological Survey of India unearthed a genuine paleolith from a small ballast pit at Pallavaram to the southward of Madras (pl. XXXIV). The correctness of the identification was soon established by a great find of similar artifacts made by Foote in the same year in company with the great geologist W. King in the gravel beds of the Kortalayar at Atrampakkam and Naranavaram rivers near Madras. Thus by one stroke the history of man in India was pushed back to a date homotaxially equivalent almost to the earliest appearance of man in Europe. A solid beginning was thus made of prehistoric studies in India.

Foote's discoveries were followed by others of equal importance. Mention may be made in this connexion of those made by C. F. Oldham in Cuddapah and North Arcot districts in 1864 and by A.B. Wynne in the Godavari valley in 1865 in association with fossil remains. About the same time Foote himself completed his survey of the Madras area down to Palar in the course of which he was able to locate a number of sites, all yielding true paleoliths. Foote later extended his investigations to other regions, and made himself the guiding spirit of prehistoric researches in the country. He was also among the first to direct attention to the pottery obtained from neolithic and megalithic sites and to understand the value to chronology of the ceramic evidence. Though these findings failed to have any immediate effect on professional archaeological thinking in the country, they were of the utmost significance for its future. There was no doubt that an entirely new world had been opened up for the student of India's past—the unknown world of the prehistoric man. It was inevitable that the discovery would force its way into the mind of the Indian archaeologist sooner or later.

A BRIEF SET-BACK AND A SWIFT RECOVERY

THE operations so brilliantly conducted by Cunningham received the highest approbation from the outside world, and particularly from Sir Charles Wood, India's first Secretary of State, who observed in his despatch dated 24 June 1864 that 'the value and importance of his investigations fully justify the anticipations which were entertained by Earl Canning, when he first conceived the idea of the survey'. Lord Lawrence's Government, however, decided to wind up the survey and these useful labours came to an abrupt termination on 9 February 1866 when Cunningham left for England.

Not that it was the intention of the Government to neglect archaeological monuments. The policy of the Government in the matter seems to have been defined in the despatch of Sir Charles Wood, dated 16 June 1866, which emphasised that 'the preservation of the historical monuments and their accurate descriptions were objects well-deserving the attention of the Government.' But this policy in actual practice did not extend beyond spasmodic official efforts in which genuine archaeological aims played very little part.

The next Secretary of State, Sir Stafford Northcote, who felt deeply exercised by the problem, addressed a private letter to Lord Lawrence emphasising the need for the preservation of architectural remains in India. The outcome of this move was that the Government issued on 29 August 1867, a circular letter to the Local Governments requiring lists to be made of all historical buildings, and photographs to be obtained of such of them as any amateur might chance to photograph. The scheme, however, failed to satisfy Sir Stafford, who directed that photographs should be prepared on a systematic basis and be accompanied by accurately drawn up plans as well as written descriptions of the subject. Soon after this, following a suggestion from the Council of Education, Science and Art Department, England, he slightly modified the scheme and proposed that casts should be made of various monuments with a view to exemplifying the different styles of Indian architecture. The expenses incurred were to be shared between the Council and the Indian Government.

The plan underwent further modifications in the hands of the Government of India, and it was finally decided that the task should be entrusted to the various Local Governments with a moderate allotment of money not exceeding Rs. 52,000 a year, and that the principals of the art colleges in India should train Indian workers to make moulds from which any requisite number of casts could be furnished. Four independent parties were proposed to conduct operations in Bombay, Madras, Bengal, and the North Western Provinces. The results following from these operations were, however, hardly commensurate with either the money, the labour or the time which was applied to them. In Bombay, thanks chiefly to the efforts of Sykes and Burgess, some good photographs and plans were produced, and a number of casts were prepared under the able supervision of Terry. The party in the Upper Provinces, led by Lt. H. H. Cole, who had been appointed the local Archaeological Surveyor, took a number of views of Kashmir, Mathura and other places, all of which were subsequently published in his *Archaeological Survey of India* (London, 1869-70). About the same time Cole also prepared a gigantic cast of the Sanchi gateway in one hundred and twelve pieces for the use of the South Kensington Museum. But the lists of monuments compiled under the scheme were generally found to be unsatisfactory. The most significant achievement of the project was the magnificent survey-operation which Rajendra Lala Mitra carried out in Orissa between 1868 and 1869 and which was later described in two monumental volumes, entitled *Antiquities of Orissa.*

The archaeological record of the period was thus, to say the least, extremely discouraging. But this was inevitable under the circumstances. The belief which dominated contemporary archaeological thinking was that only the objects which were attractive as artistic or architectural pieces, needed caring for, and that the archaeologist's function was simply to make casts or to take photographs. Among the few men in India who could see the fallacy involved in this view was E. C. Bayley, Secretary to the Home Department, who declared it to be the supreme duty of the Government not only to conserve all historical remains that had been located but to encourage the exploration of others yet to be discovered. The extent to which the latter might be brought to light was, so he felt, almost incredible, and it was his conviction that many a Pompeii was lying buried in India untouched by the archaeologist's spade.

Bayley's voice remained unheeded for the moment, and things did not change for the better till the Duke of Argyll, the new Secretary of State, directed his attention to the problem. Argyll realised at once the need for divesting the Government of the duties they had undertaken of financing desultory efforts at photographing and preparing casts, and felt persuaded that the time had arrived for directing researches in a more systematic and deliberate manner than had been attempted before. In his despatch of 11 January 1870 he advised the Government of India to make a new start for establishing a Central Department which would tackle the archaeological problem of the entire country. He also took the opportunity vehemently to denounce the prevailing tendency to rifle archaeological sites of their antiquities. He seemed to have the insight, rare all over the world in his days, to be able to perceive that antiquities were instructive when preserved in their original context. He, moreover, laid special stress on the need for conservation, pointing out that it was the bounden duty of the Government 'to prevent its own servants from wantonly accelerating the decay' of monuments.

The effect of Argyll's despatch on the Government of India was as instantaneous as it was compelling. Lord Mayo, the then Governor General, enthusiastically welcomed the proposal. 'The duty of investigating, describing and protecting the ancient monuments of a Country', he recorded in his minute of 30 May 1870, 'is recognised and acted on by every civilised nation in the world. India has done less in this direction than almost any other nation, and considering the vast materials for the illustration of history which lie unexplored in every part of Hindoostan, I am strongly of opinion that immediate steps should be taken for the creation under the Government of India of a machinery for discharging a duty, at once so obvious and so interesting' (pls. XXXV and XXXVI).

Mayo's views led to the immediate revival of the Archaeological Survey of India as a distinct department of the Government of India with a Director General as its head. The direction of the survey was again entrusted to General Cunningham. In an official resolution the task of the new Department was declared to embody 'a complete search over the whole Country, and a systematic record and description of all architectural and other remains that are either remarkable for their antiquity, or their beauty, or their historical interest'. Cunningham was further advised to address himself to the preparation of a brief summary of the labours of former investigators and of the results which had already been obtained, and to the formulation of a general scheme of a systematic enquiry for the guidance of a staff of assistants in present and future researches.

To start with, Cunningham was given a staff of two Assistants, J.D. Beglar and A. C. Carlleyle, who were later joined by H. B. W. Garrick. But the Government expressed a desire that as far as possible intelligent 'natives' should be employed in, and trained to, the task of photography, measuring and surveying buildings, directing excavations and the like and deciphering inscriptions. The Government had however no intention to set up an expensive organisation and they believed that an annual sum of £ 5,000 would be sufficient for a long time to come not only to maintain the central agency but to aid local researches and provide for the annual publications of the results attained. Even so the scheme was more liberal and more comprehensive than anything so far designed under official aegis. It reflected a clearer understanding of, and more positive approach to the archaeological needs of the country. Thus after a set-back lasting for five years archaeology at last found itself again on its feet.

CUNNINGHAM: THE SECOND PHASE

CUNNINGHAM came back to resume his interrupted task in February 1871, almost at the same time as Schliemann was preparing for his epoch-making excavations in Hissarlik. The world of archaeological thought was at that time in a state of ferment. But Cunningham appears to have been completely unaffected by it, and he preferred to adhere to his old aims and old methods. As would be clear from the memorandum drawn up by him in 1868, archaeology still connoted for him the study of architecture, sculpture, coins and inscriptions. Even the term architecture hardly suggested either to him or to any of his colleagues anything beyond monumental structures. Ordinary dwellings, the habitations of the common people, were clearly outside the scope of their programmes. The same also appears to have been the case with common artifacts–the ordinary articles of use and the tools for productive operation. None seems to have understood in those days that the aim of archaeology was to unravel the sum total of man's past achievements–to recapture his entire behaviour-pattern and that this aim could only be realised by the methodical study of his material vestiges in their entirety, whether beautiful or ugly, important or trivial.

Immediately on his arrival Cunningham applied with his two Assistants to a survey of the two great capitals of the Mughal empire, Delhi and Agra. The year 1872 was spent on tours in Rajputana, Bundelkhand, Mathura, Bodh Gaya and Gaur, while in 1873 a survey was carried out of selected sites in Panjab, in the course of which an extensive collection of Indo-Greek sculptures was obtained. Between 1873 and 1877 Cunningham traversed nearly the whole of the Central Provinces, Bundelkhand and Malwa, his first attention being directed to the magnificent stupa at Bharhut. He also succeeded in discovering several monolithic capitals and other remains of Asoka and his successors, and numerous specimens of architecture of the Gupta and the post-Gupta periods. The season of 1878-79 was devoted to further surveys in Panjab, the object of which was to complete as far as possible a general exploration of the province. The expedition was rewarded by the discovery of a huge hoard of pre-Alexandrian Indian coins at the site of Taxila.

The next season found Cunningham engaged in a tour in Bengal and Bihar, in the course of which he was able to pick up a dated inscription fixing the accession of Dharmapala of the Pala dynasty of Bengal. The year 1880-81 was spent in clearing the Bodh Gaya temple and in identifying the sites of many holy places described by the Chinese pilgrims, while the following season was devoted to a further tour in the Central Provinces. The expeditions undertaken between 1882 and 1885, which brought to a close Cunningham's exploration programme, enabled him to examine and report carefully on many historical sites in eastern Rajputana, Bundelkhand and Rewa. The results of all these labours may be aptly summed up in his own words thus :

'I have identified the sites of many of the chief cities and most famous places of ancient India, such as the rock of Aornos, the city of Taxila, and the fortress of Sangala, all connected with the history of Alexander the Great. In India I have found the sites of the celebrated cities of Sankisa, Sravasti and Kausambi, all immediately connected with the history of Buddha. Amongst other discoveries I may mention the Great Stupa of Bharhut on which most of the principal events of Buddha's life were sculptured and inscribed. I have found three dated inscriptions of King Asoka, and my assistants have brought to light a new pillar of Asoka, and a new text of his rock edicts in Bactrian characters, in which the whole of the 12th edict, which is wanting in the Shahbazgarhi text is complete.

I have traced the Gupta style of architecture in the temples of the Gupta Kings at Tigowa, Bilsar, Bhitargaon, and Deogarh, and I have discovered new inscriptions of this powerful dynasty at Eran, Udayagiri and other places.'

The discoveries which do not figure in the above summary are those which Cunningham had made in the season 1872-73 in the proto-historic site at Harappa. The extensive ruins with which the place was studded had attracted his attention as early as 1853 and again in 1856, but it was only seven years later that he made his first excavations among them. 'But the whole had been so completely cleared away by the Railway authorities' that Cunningham 'found very little worth preserving'. His 'chief discovery consisted of a number of stone implements for scraping wood or leather'. The excavations also brought to light numerous specimens of ancient pottery. 'The most curious object discovered at Harappa 'according to Cunningham was' a seal........which was found along with two small objects like chess pawns........ The seal is a smooth black stone without polish. On it is engraved very deeply a bull, without hump, looking to the right......Above the bull there is an inscription in six characters, which are quite unknown to me. They are certainly not Indian letters, and.....I conclude that the seal is foreign to India' (pls. XXXVII and XXXVIII). These are the actual words with which Cunningham disposed of the relics he had found of a great proto-historic civilisation which he never recognised for what it really was. He did not return to the subject again.

Another problem which equally escaped Cunningham's attention was that relating to the prehistoric age of India, an age which was slowly being unfolded by the labours of scientists belonging to the Geological Survey. Bruce Foote's almost sensational discovery of the first paleolith had been followed by others of hardly less importance. Among the most significant finds of the period was that obtained by Hacket in 1873, viz., a quartzite hand-axe embedded in a cliff at Bhutra on the Narmada river in association with fossil-mammalia. The find was of great assistance in determining the geological age of the Indian paleolithic folk. Although the age was still being interpreted in terms of the prevailing European nomenclature there was little doubt that a foundation had been laid for prehistoric investigations in the country.

Apart from survey and exploration of historical sites, the field which most occupied Cunningham's mind was that of the ancillary discipline of epigraphy. A number of inscriptions had already been published by scholars, but these efforts were absolutely unplanned and too few and far between, and the out-turn was altogether insignificant in comparison with the extensive materials that were available. But epigraphy received a new impetus with the founding in 1872 by James Burgess of the *Indian Antiquary*, which made possible the publication by scholars like Bühler and Fleet, Eggeling and Rice, Bhandarkar and Indraji, of many valuable inscriptions not only with texts and translations but, in many cases, with lithographic facsimiles. Cunningham's own survey-tours provided him with opportunities to pick up and examine a large number of new inscriptions which he took care to notice or publish in his survey-reports. But he felt the urge for doing the work in a more systematic and standardized manner and was persuaded that each series of inscriptions should be published in a connected form, according to the dynasties or succession of dynasties instead of being scattered, as then, over a series of different volumes and mixed up with others that had no bearing on them. The prevailing practice not only prevented the adoption of a uniform method of editing but inevitably led to duplication, the same ground being gone over again and again by different scholars working on the same inscriptions unknown to each other. Cunningham, therefore, planned to bring out a series of 'corpora' of inscriptions, the object of which was to present connected epigraphical materials in a compact and handy volume. The outcome of the plan was the appearance in 1877 of the magnificent first volume of *Corpus Inscriptionum Indicarum* embodying carefully edited texts of all the available inscriptions of Asoka and his grandson with translations and lithographic facsimiles.

But the task was already proving too great for him to cope with, and he found it necessary to entrust it to the authoritative and responsible control of a qualified full-time epigraphist. On 3 October 1881 he placed before the Government a proposal for setting up an independent epigraphical survey under the direction of J. F. Fleet, who had already become the *facile princep* in the deciphering of old inscriptions. With his usual liberality he offered to give up Rs. 500 a month of his own salary towards the pay of the new officer. Supported by James Burgess and the Berlin International Congress of Orientalists, the proposal eventually received the sanction of the Secretary of State, and Fleet was appointed on 17 January 1883 as Government Epigraphist, experimentally on a term of three years. The first duty that devolved on him was to edit the inscriptions of the Early Guptas and others connected with them, which were ultimately published in 1883 as the third volume in the series started by Cunningham. Fleet had to collect his materials all anew, in the course of which he was able to discover some entirely new inscriptions which set at rest the long-disputed question of the epoch of the Gupta era. The new volume included the finest set of lithographs that had ever yet been published and made a new starting point in the study of Indian epigraphy. The norm set by him in the editing of inscriptions is followed by Indian epigraphists even now.

So far as Persian and Arabic epigraphy was concerned Cunningham found a competent and erudite collaborator in Henry Blochmann, who had already distinguished himself by his 'Remarks on the Persian and Arabic inscription of the Bonhara mosque' (published in the *Proceedings of the Asiatic Society*, 1870), his 'Notes on the Arabic and Persian inscriptions in the Hugli district' (published in the same proceedings), and his critical studies on the inscriptions of the Muslim rulers of Bengal. To him belongs the distinction of having deciphered and published the largest number of Arabic and Persian epigraphs during the period. The greater bulk of these were furnished to him by Cunningham and his colleagues. Of the numerous epigraphical studies which stand to his credit particular mention should be made of those compiled by him on the inscriptions of Delhi, Mahoba, Ajmer, Agra, Sikandra, Jaunpur, Rohtas, Sasaram, to give only a few items, all having been published between 1872 and 1878.

Conservation was, from the very first, kept outside the Director General's purview. But on 13 February 1873 the Central Government issued a circular assigning to Local Governments the duty of caring for the preservation of all buildings and monuments of historical and architectural interest. A different emphasis, however, came to be placed on imperial responsibility in this respect when Lord Lytton took up the reins of the Viceregal office. One of his first endeavours was to prevent the despoiling of the archaeological remains by treasure-hunters, and the outcome was the Treasure Trove Act of 1878, which authorized the Government to claim possession of any treasure unearthed that exceeded ten rupees in value. In January 1878 Lytton recorded in a minute that 'the preservation of the national antiquities and works of art ought not to be exclusively left to the charge of Local Governments, which may not always be alive to the importance of such a duty. Lieutenant Governors who combined aesthetic culture with administrative energy are not likely to be very common, and I cannot conceive of any claims upon the administrative and financial resources of the Supreme Government more essentially imperial than this'.

Lytton followed this up with a resolution drafted in the same year recommending the appointment of a Curator of Ancient Monuments, who was to carry out under the Central Government a general system of conservation. He was to prepare classified lists of the monuments of each province, grouping lists of them according as they required to be kept in permanent good repair or were decayed beyond that point but still not in complete ruin or were unimportant or irretrievably ruined. The Central Government were then to arrange with each Local Government for the grant to be made to the latter for the preservation of the monuments in aid of local resources. All provincial projects for repair and restoration were to be submitted to the Centre through the Curator, points of architectural taste being referred to a Committee of Taste, to be set up under the scheme. The proposal, though negatived by the Secretary of State in 1878 on the ground that the scrutiny of provincial projects could be equally well done by the Director General of Archaeology and that the proposed Curator was an unnecessary fifth wheel in the coach, was revived under Lord Ripon in a slightly modified form, and the appointment of a special officer as Curator of Ancient Monuments was sanctioned on 11 November 1880 for a term of three years.

Major H.H. Cole was the officer selected for the new post, and he joined his duties in January 1881. His task was 'to give the Government of India and the Local Governments the advantage of professional advice concerning the restoration and conservation of ancient monuments throughout India', the Local Governments being left to provide a permanent system of inspection and conservation. Earlier, in April 1880, Cole had been appointed on the special duty of examining the condition of the monuments of Lahore, Delhi and Agra and had compiled an excellent report of the work done. He had great knowledge of his subject, great industry and great enthusiasm, and during the three years allotted to him he was able to examine nearly all the most important buildings in British India and the Indian States and to draw up valuable lists and memoranda of work to be done, which were later appended to his three gigantic reports (published in 1882, 1883 and 1885). Cole also produced in twenty-two parts a series of Preliminary Reports on particular groups of monuments in Bombay, Madras, Rajputana, Hyderabad, Panjab and the North-Western Provinces. He personally supervised the repairs of quite a large number of these buildings, and under his aegis many useful restorations were effected in the gateway at Sanchi, in the fort at Agra, in Akbar's tomb at Sikandra, at Fatehpur Sikri, Mathura and Brindavan.

Cole suffered, however, from a tendency to go beyond his special field of work and take part in activities which had no bearing on conservation. He actually embarked on archaeleogical survey and excavation-operations and projected a costly scheme of publication, which in the end had to be stopped under Government orders. The materials, which contained exceptionally fine illustrations of the most famous buildings surveyed by him, were subsequently distributed in ten folio volumes without title-page. When his term lapsed in 1883, the appointment was abolished, and the Government decided to revert to the old system of leaving the task of conservation to Local Governments.

The new decision was communicated to the Local Governments in a Resolution dated 26 November 1883. The latter were required to take up on the basis of Cole's Report for 1882-83 the preparation of a classified list showing separately : (1) the monuments which from their 'present condition' and historical or archaeological value ought to be kept in permanent good repairs; (2) those which it was only possible or desirable to save from further decay by such minor measures as the eradication of vegetation, the exclusion of water from the walls or the like; and (3) those which for their advanced stage of decay or comparative unimportance it was impossible or unnecessary to preserve. Due provision was to be made for the proper custody and keeping up of the monuments in classes I and II, the cost being charged to the public works allotment of each province. Only in very special cases would the Government of India promise further assistance from the imperial funds. But when all the lists eventually came to be submitted, they were found to be drawn up on such very dissimilar plans that a satisfactory amalgamation was unpracticable, and the Government had to send them back for being revised according to the form prescribed by them.

The exclusion of conservation from the scope of the Archaeological Survey brought forth comments from Cunningham who believed that 'the trained and experienced archaeologist who has examined and measured and described the buildings of different ages was naturally the best authority as to the style of all the repairs that may be required for any ancient monuments'. He pointed out that the divided authority was a mistake and that the only judicious arrangement was the combination of conservation with exploration.

But Cunningham had in the meantime decided to retire. He had put up almost eighteen year's continuous labour and felt satisfied that the greater part of north India had been fully explored and that the time had arrived when the survey organization itself could be dissolved without any loss to archaeology. He believed that the future work of exploration could be successfully carried out by a much smaller and less expensive establishment. He accordingly recommended the abolition of the Director General's post and the reorganization of north India into three independent circles—Panjab with Sind and Rajputana, the North-Western Provinces (present Uttar Pradesh) with the Central India Agency and the Central Provinces; and Bengal including Bihar, Orissa, Assam and Chota Nagpur, each being managed by a separate Surveyor with a small staff of two assistants and two draftsmen. Madras with Bombay and Hyderabad was to be left to the charge of Burgess, the then archaeological Surveyor of the area, while epigraphy was to remain, as at that time, to be dealt with by Fleet. The Surveyors were to be on the footing of professional advisers to the Local Governments and the Political Agencies, to which they were required to send their reports and programmes of work, and which they were also to advise as to the various monuments and buildings which required to be restored or preserved.

These recommendations were accepted by the Government with the only modification that the new Surveyors should submit their reports on the strictly survey-part of their work through Burgess. Under the new arrangement Bengal was entrusted to Cunningham's assistant, Beglar, and the North-Western Provinces to Major J. B. Keith, who had as his assistant Dr. A. Führer, then Curator, Lucknow Museum, while the Panjab Circle was placed under C. J. Rodgers.

Cunningham's retirement on 1 October 1885 deprived the Indian archaeological scene of its most colourful figure, a colossus which had been bestriding it for over a quarter of a century. His contribution to the development of Indian archaeology has been vigorously disputed. To some he was the father of Indian archaeology, who had by his ceaseless labours given form and precision to aims and methods which had before him been only hazy and elusive. To others he was only a remarkable amateur whose reputation derived from the astonishing value and interest of his finds and who remained to the last ignorant of all the scientific methods, which, during the period of his sway, had forced their way into the mind of the western and the near eastern archaeologists. Archaeology with him was but a search for past architectural styles, art-treasures, coins and inscriptions, and its connection with the study of the common objects which consisted of man's material culture ever eluded his grasp, although this connection had been firmly established by the works of Thomsen, Worsaae and Nilsson in Denmark, of Giuseppe Fiorelli in Italy, and of Curtius, Dörpfeld and Schliemann in Greece and Anatolia.

The excavations undertaken by Cunningham seldom went beyond what might be called prospecting. A very considerable number of stupas were no doubt opened, rifled of their deposits and searched for inscriptions; and surface-diggings and small clearings were effected in many of the ancient mounds and fields of ruins. But rarely did he undertake deep or extensive excavation, and such of it as was attempted, as at Gaya, Sanchi, Taxila and Bhilsa, did more harm than good by its consistent neglect of stratigraphical principles leading inevitably to the destruction of much archaeological evidence. To the claims of prehistory he remained indifferent to the end, and in the megalithic monuments, which the conjoined labours of Babington and Harkness, Congreve and Kearnes, Newbold and Meadows Taylor had brought to light, he was disposed to see only an earlier form of the stupa. Even more surprising is the apathy he evinced towards palaeoliths, the occurrence of which in India had been established beyond doubt by Bruce Foote and his colleagues of the Geological Survey during the early sixties of the century. Cunningham, as we have seen, was within an ace of an epoch-making discovery in 1873, when he unearthed at Harappa a pictographic seal along with many specimens of Harappan pottery. But he scarcely understood that they were the fragments of a great past civilization. He touched it, but passed it by.

Yet, it would be nothing short of squeamishness to scan Cunningham for faults which he shared with all his colleagues in India and with many in the west. No one with any archaeological experience can refuse to acknowledge the value of his great pioneering work. He was one of the first to stress the importance of field-work, accurate description and precise measurement, and he shared with Prinsep the honour of liberating archaeology of its literary and antiquarian affiliations. His ideal of survey-work was comprehensive enough to include every site that was of promise, every antiquity that was of interest, and he was responsible for evolving a uniform system of recording under which the description of each building was to be accompanied by an account of its history and purpose, of its mode of construction, of the nature and colour of its material and even of the mason's marks on the stones. Above all, he was prompt in publishing his results, as is amply testified by the twentythree volumes of his survey-reports, which, in Lord Curzon's picturesque words, 'constitute........a noble mine of information in which the student has but to delve in order to discover an abundant spoil'.

JAMES BURGESS

CUNNINGHAM'S activities were exclusively confined to North India. He had no time to direct his attention to the archaeological problems relating to the other parts of the country. The man who endeavoured to fill this blank in Cunningham's programme as far as it affected west and south India was James Burgess, (pl. V) whose keen interest in the antiquities of these regions and early training as an architect had eminently fitted him for this significant role. When, in 1873, a regular archaeological survey was for the first time constituted for west India, the charge of its operation was appropriately entrusted to Burgess, who had by that date compiled not only an extensive inventory of principal monuments in Bombay, Sind, Berar, the Central Provinces and Hyderabad, but had, in addition to a monograph on Elephanta, brought out three portfolios of photographs dealing with the Satrunjaya temples, the monuments of Somnath, Junagadh, and Girnar and the ancient architecture of Gujarat and Ahmedabad. The new arrangement was sanctioned for three years, subsequently extended to five, at an annual cost of Rs. 13,000. There was no provision for a permanent staff, and Burgess was required to conduct his field-work for six months of cold season each year, at the end of which he was to dismiss his assistants and take the materials to England for publication.

Burgess started his operations on 15 January 1874, covering in his first season everything of interest in Belgaum and Kaladgi districts. The next season was devoted to Kathiawad and Cutch, and the season of 1875-76 to the western districts of the Nizam's dominions, the results of all these operations being published in three magnificent volumes of reports with numerous photographic and other illustrations Burgess' fourth volume embodied a report on the Buddhist cave-temples in the Deccan, representing the result of his operations during 1876-79. On the expiry of his five-year term in 1879 Burgess found that he had covered only a small fraction of his programme. He asked for a further extension of four years and also pressed for a permanent staff that would carry on field-work during his absence in England. The extension was agreed to, but the Government met his other demand only halfway by providing for the appointment of an assistant on a year-to-year basis.

In November 1881 the scope of Burgess' activities underwent a radical expansion by the amalgamation with his existing charge that of the newly constituted Archaeological Survey of South India. A proposal for organizing a regular survey in the south had been in the air since about 1874, when the Secretary of State addressed a letter on the subject to the Provincial Government. Delays, however, had intervened, and nothing substantial had been done in the province beyond the appointment of Robert Sewell of the Provincial Civil Service for conducting the exploration of the Amaravati stupa and for the compilation of a basic list of all antiquarian remains in the Presidency. Sewell's lists of antiquarian remains and report on the Amaravati excavations carried out in 1877 thus formed the foundation on which Burgess was called upon to build. But Burgess was equal to the challenge, and in his first season he was able to complete the survey of the remains round Vijayawada and the Amaravati and Jaggayyapeta stupas, combining with this task a thorough examination of the Chalukyan temples in Dharwar district. In 1882 his burden was somewhat lightened by the appointment of Alexander Rea as his assistant, in collaboration with whom he was able to bring to completion not only the survey which he had taken up of the Maḍura district but also the examination already undertaken of the monuments in the Belgaum region. In 1883-84, while Rea surveyed in detail the remains at Mahabalipuram and the ruins at Hampi, Burgess directed his attention to the Muslim architecture at Champaner, Dholka and Ahmedabad.

The next year was devoted to the survey of Dabhoi, Cambay and Broach and to the study of the Pallava temples at Kanchi. Burgess had by then been able to make a better assessment of the magnitude and complexity of his task and had felt convinced that for west India alone, exclusive of Sind, there were six more year's work ahead and that to complete the work it was essential that the staff under him should be sanctioned on a permanent basis. For Madras he found it more difficult to make an estimate, but he suggested that the work should be continued for a further term of five years, that the staff should be given a regular scale of pay and that an epigraphist well-versed in Sanskrit, Pali and the Dravidian languages should be employed on translating inscriptions in these languages, to enable the Survey to complete its work 'within a reasonable time'. The scheme was approved by the Government of India for a term of five years, and Dr. E. Hultzsch, an eminent linguist, was selected for the post of Epigraphist in August 1886 on the basis of a three-year contract.

While the survey machine in the south and the west was being put in order, Burgess was invited by the Government to fill Cunningham's place in north India by becoming the channel for the submission of the reports from the three new survey-circles. Burgess, however, had no desire to accept his predecessor's position without his powers and pointed out that the new system would not work unless it was placed under him in name as well as in fact. With the solitary exception of Führer, then in temporary charge of the North-Western Provinces, none of the new Surveyors, in his view, had either the scholarship, experience or training essential for the direction of survey-work, and even Führer lacked architectural training which was a serious drawback. Each one of them, therefore, required detailed professional supervision almost at every stage.

Burgess, moreover, found the system unncessarily expensive and believed that substantial economy could be effected by retrenching some of the higher posts and employing instead a larger number of lower-paid assistants. He suggested the abolition of the Epigraphist's office, which was costing Government Rs. 20,000 annually without yielding, in his view, an adequate return, and he assured the Government that with a much smaller grant of Rs. 7,000 he would be able to get accomplished what Fleet was doing with the help of the most competent scholars in India and Europe. As a further step both to efficiency and economy, Burgess recommended complete amalgamation of conservation with survey-work and pleaded for closer co-operation between the museums and survey officers in the matter of conserving, describing and studying the antiquities unearthed by the latter.

All these recommendations bore fruit in an official decision to unify under a single executive head not only the three separate Surveys in the north, west and south but of the three distinct fields of operation popularly associated with archaeology : exploration, conservation and epigraphy. But the unification, remained no more than a distant ideal, and the machinery devised to implement it left little initiative or power in the hands of the Director General. No report or programme could reach him from any of his colleagues before it had been scrutinized by the appropriate Local Administration, whose suggestions he had no authority either to alter or to set aside without reference to the Centre. Programmes of conservation were to be drawn up by the regional Surveyors and to be submitted to the local authorities for their decisions. The Director General was to act only as a post-office; he could offer his comments but take no decision. At Burgess' suggestion, however, the Assistant Surveyor's post in the Panjab Circle was retrenched and E.W. Smith was appointed as Architectural Assistant in the North-Western Provinces to fill the gaps in Führer's qualifications. With the termination of Fleet's appointment on 1 June 1886, epigraphy also came under the control of the Survey and an annual grant of Rs. 6,000 was placed at its disposal to enable the deciphering, the translation and the publication of ancient inscriptions.

Burgess' first task as Director General, whose duties he assumed on 25 March 1886, was to obtain the details which, in his view, the northern Surveys had neglected in respect of architectural measurements and drawings. His aims and methods hardly differed from Cunningham's except in the added emphasis he preferred to place on architectural survey. 'Archaeology being', in his view, 'but the history of art', he considered it to be his aim 'to provide a pretty full illustration and history of ancient and medieval architecture down to the decline of the Muhammedan styles'. To this one end he subordinated most of his programmes, as would be amply evidenced by the nature and the quality of the careful architectural surveys carried out either by him or by his colleagues during the eventful years covering his stewardship.

Among the most outstanding of these activities was the elaborate survey made by Führer and Smith between 1886 and 1887 of the Sharqi architecture of Jaunpur and of the monuments of Zafarabad, Saheth Maheth and Ayodhya. Equally noteworthy were the operations conducted by Smith during 1888-89 in Budaon, Lalitpur, Orchha and other places in Bundelkhand, the survey of ancient architecture in north Gujarat and the Muslim architecture in Bijapur carried out by Henry Cousens, and that of the monuments at Mahabalipuram and of the antiquities in Krishna, Nellore and Godavari districts completed by Rea during the same period. Burgess found hardly any time to take much active interest in excavation, and the only major operation undertaken by him was the digging up of the Kankali Tila mound at Mathura, between 1887 and 1888. Yet, this in itself was a great achievement, as the effect of the excavation, which brought to light a plethora of sculptures bearing dated inscriptions, was not only to open up a new world for the Indian archaeologist but to make him for the first time alive to the value of deep and extensive digging.

But Burgess did more than this. Although he was ignorant of the scientific techniques available in his time, he was clear-sighted enough to insist on a professional control of excavation and to press for official measures that would illegalize any digging, except those which the Archaeological Survey itself conducted. He was also the first man to devote himself strenuously to the task of ridding India of robbers and art-collection touts masquerading as antiquarians. In 1886 he succeeded in inducing the Government to issue two directives, one debarring public officers from disposing of, without official approval, antiquities found or acquired by them; the other forbidding the digging up of ancient remains of any kind without the previous consent of the Archaeological Survey. Burgess wanted to follow this up by an amendment of the Treasure Trove Act which would make it unlawful to export antiquities without an official permit; but nothing tangible came out of this laudable endeavour.

To the field of epigraphy Burgess rendered a signal service by starting in October 1888 a quarterly publication *Epigraphia Indica*, of which he was able to bring out, in two year's time, as many as eight fascicules containing highly valuable inscriptions edited by great epigraphists like Bühler, Kielhorn and Eggeling. Earlier he had compiled a volume of Tamil and Sanskrit inscriptions and his colleague E. Hultzsch, collected and edited a mass of south Indian epigraphic records sufficient to fill three large volumes. A good feature of Burgess' archaeological administration was that he laid special emphasis on the enlisting of native talents in the discovery and translation of inscriptions and training them up in the technique of epigraphical researches.

In bringing out the results of his investigations Burgess followed a system somewhat different from Cunningham's. Instead of publishing periodical reports of his discoveries at the time they were made, he preferred to keep his materials with him till enough had been collected and studied to enable the production of a complete monograph that would present an exhaustive and authoritative treatment of the subject under enquiry. By this means he was able, within fifteen years, starting from his first assumption of duties in western India, to produce no less than twenty magnificent volumes, of which seven formed part of the *Archaeological Survey of India, New Imperial Series.* But he was attempting what was perhaps beyond the capacity of any single man, and in February 1889, about eighteen months before his due date of retirement, he found himself encumbered with a huge mass of material sufficient to fill twelve large volumes in the *New Imperial Series* and one of the *Epigraphia Indica.* Criticized for the 'arrears,' and convinced that there was no prospect of liquidating them by the scheduled date, Burgess withdrew from service on 1 June 1889 to be able to concentrate on the publication work.

For the future arrangement of archaeological work in the country Burgess submitted a plan to the Government, in which he estimated that the survey of south

India would need about eight years to complete and that of west India a year's time only, while more than five year's work awaited the archaeologists in each of the four areas into which he would like to see the rest of the country archaeologically divided; viz., Rajputana with Sind, Panjab, Central India, and the North-Western Provinces with Oudh. Bengal was omitted, as it was considered to have already been satisfactorily surveyed. There was no necessity in his view to maintain an elaborate machinery for carrying on the residuary work, and he suggested the retrenchment of the Director General's office and the reduction of the entire Survey to two independent parties, one working under Cousens and the other under Rea. The Panjab and Bengal Surveys were to be eliminated altogether, and the services of Cousens and Rea were to be made available for operations in the north as soon as they could be spared from the work they had in hand. For the whole of north India he wanted an additional 'architectural archaeologist', who, besides conducting minor surveys, would be responsible for conservation work. He also urged that Hultzsch should continue to be in charge of south Indian epigraphy, but on an enhanced scale of pay, while Führer should be retained in the North-Western Provinces as a general antiquarian and epigraphist to provide the complement of Hultzsch's work for north India.

The scheme received a ready welcome from the Government, who, influenced by the adverse comment of the Finance Committee on the high cost of archaeology, had already agreed in 1888 to a policy of drastic reductions. The new policy led to the virtual disappearance of the Archaeological Survey as a central body and was a reversion to the chaos and disorganization of the pre-Cunningham era. The whole of India was denuded of its archaeological staff, barring two Surveyors in the west and the south, raised now to the status of Superintendents pursuing their separate aims independently of each other, and a third, Führer, who was entrusted with the vague duties of general antiquarian and epigraphical research and whose relations with the other Surveys remained ill-defined. Even Burgess' proposal for an architect-curator for north India was rejected, and E.W. Smith, whom he had nominated for the post, was placed under Führer as his assistant. Not only the work of conservation but the entire executive direction of survey-operations relapsed into the hands of the Provincial Governments. The only redeeming feature of the new system was the retention of Hultzsch as the Government Epigraphist in Madras for a further term of three years, but his office was made independent of the south Indian survey. Even in this drastically reduced shape the Survey-establishments were sanctioned only for five years (from the 1st October 1890), and Lord Cross, the Secretary of State, while approving of the scheme, expressed the hope that by the end of that period the survey-work would, so far as the Government was concerned, be generally completed.

With Burgess ended the era of what he himself used to term 'architectural archaeology.' Archaeology was for him mainly a search for architectural styles—a hunt for the evidence that might reveal the age, the purpose and the history of a structure, as also the arrangement and the relations of the sculptures associated with it. Artefacts other than *objets d'art* were outside the scope of his investigations. This was no doubt too narrow a view of the functions of archaeology. But this also happened to be a view which he shared with most of his contemporaries. And when all is said, it is difficult to over-estimate the substantial services he had rendered not only in the field of architectural survey but in the conservation of historical monuments.

A BLEAK INTERLUDE

THE period immediately following Burgess' retirement was one of almost unrelieved gloom, during which archaeology found itself caught up again in stagnant waters. On the credit side one could of course show Burgess' own attractive publications on the Muslim architecture of Gujarat and Ahmedabad and the brilliant achievements of some of his successors, particularly of Führer at Kankali Tila and of E.W. Smith at Agra and Fatehpur Siki. But these by themselves could hardly inspire any optimism about the future of archaeology in the country. It is true that epigraphy continued to make progress under the able direction of Hultzsch, who brought out more volumes of south Indian inscriptions and that the *Epigraphia Indica*, after Burgess had relinquished its charge in 1892, was given a fresh lease of life by arranging to issue it under Hultzsch's editorship as a supplement to the *Indian Antiquary*. But this was done as a strictly temporary measure in the hope that the work would be completed by the end of Hultzsch's term. The hope, however, seemed as distant as ever, and Hultzsch's term, which expired in 1893, had to be further extended for five years.

Conservation hardly fared better except perhaps in the North Western Provinces where, thanks chiefly to the personal initiative of a succession of able Lieutenant Governors, a vigorous repair-programme was being pursued. Listing of monuments continued to be far behind the schedule, and where such lists existed they were often found to be incomplete or defective.

But it was excavation which was to suffer worst of all under the new arrangement. No serious attention was directed to the task and both archaeologists and officials who were responsible for shaping archaeological policy seemed to be labouring under the belief that everything that required to be done in the way of exploration or excavation had already been completed or was well-nigh completion, and there were no residual problems remaining to be tackled. This policy, or lack of policy, drew forth well-merited protests from scholars both in and outside India, who were more well-posted about the nature as well as the magnitude of the task awaiting the archaeologist. Rudolf Hoernle, for instance, felt deeply perturbed by the fact that in the field of excavation 'nothing whatsoever has been done' by Indian archaeology, although it formed 'the essential part of any properly conducted archaeological survey' and 'its results are of the utmost importance from the historical point of view.' He pointed out with regret that 'in 1862.......the late Sir A. Cunningham enumerated 20 places as pre-eminently deserving exploration. Three of these are......Vaisali, Patna (the Palibothra) and Rajgir, three of the most important capital towns of the time of Buddha. Though more than 30 years have passed since then, and the archaeological survey of India is supposed to be complete, not one of the three ancient sites has been explored or their details even definitely identified'.

Georg Bühler, who joined his voice to that of Hoernle, regretted that despite the enormous mass of materials which the work of Cunningham, Burgess and their successors had brought to light, the world still knew hardly anything about India's past beyond the age of Asoka. The only way to recover the earlier history of the country, he pointed out, was to dig deep and to excavate in a methodical and scientific manner the sites of all old centres of the religious and political life of India. He deprecated the idea of limiting activities to Buddhist sites only. The sites, which in his view were likely to be rewarding, included, among others, Patna, Kosam, Ujjain, Ahichchhatra, Peukelaotis (Charsadda), Taxila and Mathura. Many years later each one of these sites was to yield an amazingly rich crop of archeological finds. But the Government of the day did not evince any interest in them, and Hoernle and Bühler and other scholars who shared their view went on crying in the wilderness.

When, at last, in 1895 the Government of India came to take stock of the situation, they were almost frightened by the sheer volume of the work remaining to be done. On a suggestion from the Secretary of State they had already made a move to transfer the entire work to the Asiatic Society of Bengal. But the latter refused to accept the responsibility, and the Government were forced to the view that the direction of archaeological work by private enterprise was out of the question, and that the work must be continued by the Government if it was to continue at all. The matter was debated for a considerable time, in the course of which they were able to weigh the views not only of the Provincial Governments but of such learned bodies as the Royal Asiatic Society and scholars like Tawney, Bühler and Fleet, and it was not until 1898 that they were in a position to submit for the consideration of the Secretary of State their final proposals for the reorganization of archaeological work in India.

In the scheme that was drawn up, provision was made for five circles with an Archaeological Surveyor in charge of each, viz., Bombay with Sind and Berar; Madras and Coorg; Panjab, Baluchistan and Ajmer; North-Western Provinces and Central Provinces; Bengal and Assam. The machinery of the Central Government being considered unsuitable for executive supervision, the Surveyors were placed under the control of the Local Governments first named in the circle-designations thus devised, while the Survey expenditure was charged to the imperial revenues except in the case of Madras, where, since 1890, it had been a provincial charge. The new survey circles were required to devote themselves entirely to conservation-work, which, in the Government's view, was the first aim of archaeology. Excavation they viewed as only a secondary objective, and they announced that the limited funds they were justified in spending should primarily be applied to the preservation of existing materials rather than to the exploration of what was unknown.

The new scheme, however, made a much more generous provision for epigraphy, though the Government's original idea had been to keep in abeyance the post of Epigraphist and the publication of the *Epigraphia Indica* and to relegate the work to private enterprise. But the latter view was so strongly contested both by Local Governments and by private authority that it had ultimately to be abandoned. The Madras Government pointed out that Dr. Hultzsch and his staff were the only people living who were able to decipher the old Tamil inscriptions and that epigraphy was not only a subject of scientific interest and importance in which the learned alone were much interested but also one which might throw useful light on many problems of administration. It was, therefore, decided to make the post of Epigraphist permanent so long as Dr. Hultzsch continued to hold it. But as he was emphatically a specialist in the south Indian inscriptions, the Government proposed to encourage the appointment of honorary epigraphists in other provinces and to relax Hultzsch's editorial monopoly by authorizing them to edit inscriptions for publication in the *Epigraphia Indica.*

The whole of the scheme was sanctioned by the Secretary of State on 18 May 1899. One good feature of it was that it made service in the Archaeological Survey pensionable for all who had joined the Survey before that date. But it suffered from a number of defects. It completely ignored the value of excavation and left all initiative and responsibility in the hands of the Local Governments, particularly in respect of conservation. The Survey was allowed to remain without any kind of leadership whatever.

In this picture of general gloom the only silver lining was presented by an event which took place in 1891 and which proved to be of the utmost significance to archaeological discoveries many years later. In that year Sir Charles Close (then a lieutenant in the Survey of India) suggested that balloons fitted with cameras should be used for photographing archaeological sites near Agra. The scheme received the approval of the Surveyor General of India, but eventually yielded no more than a few aerial photographs, none of which related to archaeological sites. Close's plan to have a bird's eye overall view of the cultural landscape around Agra remained no more than a dream which met its fulfilment only after the end of the second world war. The idea, in fact, was too revolutionary to excite any active interest among his contemporaries.

CURZON AND THE DAWN OF A NEW ERA

FROM the stagnancy which, towards the close of the nineteenth century, seemed to threaten the very existence of Indian archaeology, it was saved by the almost providential arrival on the scene of Lord Curzon of Kedleston, Governor General of India from 1899-1905 (pl. VI). In Curzon the intellectual awakening set in motion by the provocative writings of Bühler, Hoernle and others found its ablest and most enthusiastic champion. While still in England, he had been deeply shocked by the extremely barren and unimaginative policy which the Government of India had been pursuing in archaeological matters, and one of the first tasks he undertook immediately on his setting foot in India was to commence a personal study of the existing system in every province of India. By September 1900 he had gathered in his hands enough material to convince him that 'it was impossible to conceive a system more chaotic or futile in practice.' His findings on the subject and the views he arrived at on their basis may be read in the extracts given below of a minute he recorded on 23 September:

'I cannot conceive any obligation more strictly appertaining to a Supreme Government than the Conservation of the most beautiful and perfect collection of monuments in the world, or one more likely to be scamped and ignored by a delegation of all authority to provincial administrations........

'The whole country is supposed to be divided into five circles with an Archaeological Surveyor for each. The geographical arrangement of these circles is fantastic in the extreme. Sind is lumped together with Bombay and Berar; Baluchistan is tacked on to the Punjab, and Ajmer is casually thrown in. The Central Provinces are added to the North Western Provinces........Bengal......has no surveyor. The surveyors in the remaining circles, instead of being scholars, or even engineers, are merely as their name implies—surveyors, who make drawings, and write reports but can only at a considerable risk be entrusted with the task of renovation of repair.

'In practice, too, the most whimsical difference prevails between the policy adopted in different Provinces. No Local Government is *per se* interested in archaeology. It is occupied with grosser and more material concerns. The result is that the progress or suspension of archaeological work, the decay of priceless treasures of art, the restoration, sometimes involving the prostitution of exquisite palaces and halls—all depend upon the taste, or interest, or caprice of the Local Governor, who, if in a few rare cases he exerts himself in the cause of art and good taste, may on the other hand, if he chose, leave an indelible and fatal mark upon the monuments of his province, or more frequently, be content with leaving no mark at all.

'Thus it has come about that owing to the absence of any central and duly qualified advising authority, not merely are beautiful and famous buildings crumbling to decay; but there is neither principle nor unity in conservation or repair, while from time to time horrors are still committed that make the student shudder and turn grey

'The continuance of this state of affairs seems to me little short of a scandal. Were Germany the ruling power in India, I do not hesitate to say that she would be spending many lakhs a year on a task to what we have hitherto rather plumed ourselves on our generosity in devoting Rs. 61,000, raised only a little more than a year ago to 88,000.......

'When I reflect upon the sums of money that are gaily dispensed on the construction of impossible forts in impossible places, which are to sustain an impossible siege against an impossible foe, I do venture to hope that so mean a standard may not again be pleaded, at any rate in my time.'

These noble reflections found concrete expression in a set of definite proposals submitted to the Secretary of State on 20 December 1900, the chief of which was to eliminate the existing lack of responsibility and system. Arguing for the proposals Curzon's Government pointed out that it was indefensible that the Government should divest themselves of all responsibilities for the preservation of monuments, which, in the words of Lord Lytton, were 'for variety, extent, completeness and beauty unsurpassed, perhaps unequalled in the world', and that the Government of India, not the Local Administrations, would always be held in the judgement of the civilized world primarily responsible for maintaining intact this great inheritance. They considered it unsafe to trust that the subordinate governments would always be willing or able under the pressing exigencies of provincial finance to devote funds to it. They were satisfied that the existing Archaeological Surveyors were insufficiently equipped with archaeological scholarly or professional knowledge to act as independent advisers or investigators and that they required to be guided and controlled if their activities were to lead to any useful results.

The Government, therefore, recommended the revival of the post of the Director General, the incumbent of which was to be a trained explorer combining archaeological knowledge with engineering skill. He was required to exercise a general supervision over all the archaeological work of the country, whether it was that of excavation, of preservation or of repair, of epigraphy, or of the registration and description of monuments and ancient remains. He would coordinate and bring up-to-date the local surveys and reports and should in addition present to Government an annual report of his work.

The Government also pressed for an annual sum of a lakh of rupees for a term of years to be expended in grants-in-aid for the archaeological work of special importance and magnitude. In pleading for this grant they observed that they could furnish 'a multitude of cases in which beautiful or famous fabrics are crumbling away to ruin, partly from the lack of authoritative supervision or control, still more from the reluctance or inability of the local Government to assume a burden which is entirely optional and may be repudiated with equanimity....A process of restoration commenced under one regime is suspended or abandoned by its successor. Buildings which it is still possible to save are fast slipping into irrepairable decay. In fact we must confess that there is at present a total lack both of responsibility and system . . Learned scholars, particularly from the European

Continent, seldom come to this country without publishing sharp attacks upon the Government.... for its presumed apathy and indifference. Even the native press has begun to take a keen interest in the monuments of Indian antiquity and calls loudly for a more consistent and a more liberal policy. We believe that there is no object upon which the annual expenditure of such a small sum as we propose will be more unanimously endorsed by public opinion in this Country.'

The proposals were sanctioned by the Secretary of State on 29 November 1901 experimentally for a five-year term, and, on a recommendation from the British Museum, John Marshall (knighted in 1914) who had already worked in Greece, South Turkey and Crete, was selected for filling the new post of Director General (pl. VII). In the Resolution (dated 21 February 1902) announcing the appointment it was declared that the most important function of the Director General was to secure that the ancient monuments of the country were properly cared for, that they were not utilized for purposes which were inappropriate or unseemly, that repairs were executed when required and that any restoration which might be attempted were conducted on artistic lines. He was to assist the regional Surveyors in ascertaining and formulating the special requirements of each province and to advise the Government of India as to the operations for which subsidies might be allotted from imperial funds. He was to visit all the circles in succession, succinctly reporting the general results of his tour to the Government of each province visited and offering any suggestion that he might have to make in connexion with the buildings he had inspected. He was, finally, to exercise a professional control over all his colleagues and to maintain a continuous record of the needs of the various provinces and of the action taken to meet them.

Although conservation was accorded the first place in the new programme, Lord Curzon was clear-sighted enough to visualize that 'it is in the exploration and study of purely Indian remains, in the probing of the archaic mounds, in the excavation of old Indian cities and in the copying and reading of ancient inscriptions that a good deal of the.....work of the archaeologists will in future live'. 'Epigraphy', he announced in a speech delivered before the Asiatic Society of Bengal on 6 February 1900, 'should not be set behind research any more than research should be set behind conservation. All are ordered parts of any scientific scheme of antiquarian work. I am not one of those who think that Government can afford to patronize the one and ignore the other. It is in my judgement equally our duty to dig and discover, to classify, reproduce and describe, to copy and decipher and to cherish and conserve.'

Such then was the mighty task which Curzon had mapped out for the reconstituted Archaeological Survey. It was not all his fault that all the means, in men as well as money, required to implement it could not be made available to the new Director General, who was, in addition, burdened with a cumbersome administrative machine derived from an impossible system which it had been the Viceroy's most cherished desire totally to scrap. The actual work of conservation, as in the days of Burgess, was still wholly in the hands of the Provincial Governments whom the Director General could advise but could not guide. The regional surveyors were under his control only professionally, but administratively they continued to be accountable to the Local Administrations. The picture was indeed very different from what the Viceroy had conceived in his Minutes and speeches.

But Curzon had to fight against many heavy odds, and it is not surprising that he failed to overcome many of the prejudices inherited from a long established tradition. Many of his colleagues did not see eye to eye with him, and even the authorities in England were strongly opposed to complete centralisation. One should not, moreover, be too squeamish. Curzon had to accept the scheme as finally approved despite the holes which it only too glaringly displayed. All the same he had fought and won one of the most difficult battles ever waged for Indian archaeology. No other ruler of India before or after him has evinced so single-minded a devotion to the cause of archaeology, and, when all is said, it has to be admitted that he succeded in rekindling an archaeological conscience in the country and placing the Archaeological Survey of India for the first time on a sound and secure foundation.

Curzon's work did not, however, cease after he had provided this foundation. He knew that it could only be gradually built upon and that many years' efforts would be required before a solid and imposing structure could be raised on it. But he himself materially aided this task of building up by simultaneously pushing through a number of reforms, each of which was basic to the functioning of the survey apparatus he had set up. One of these reforms consisted in bringing within the purview of the survey the archaeological work in the then existing Indian States. As a consequence of this measure Kashmir, Rajputana and the Panjab States, as well as, Dir, Swat, and Chitral, were included in the Panjab Circle; Baroda, Central India, Hyderabad (Deccan) were added to the Bombay Circle; while Madras and Bengal States were brought within the purview of the Bengal and Madras Circles respectively.

All these had been effected by 1901. But further changes came in 1902 when steps were taken to appoint a separate officer to take care of Muslim architectural remains in North India, and the entire archaeological work of the United Provinces, barring the protection of architecture, was shifted to the Panjab Circle. About the same time it was decided to transfer Rajputana and the Central Provinces from the latter Circle to Bombay.

These organisational achievements were, however, overshadowed by a reform of much greater significance, viz., the enactment of the Ancient Monuments Preservation Act of 1904. The main objects of the Act were: to ensure the proper upkeep and repair of ancient buildings in private ownership excepting such as were used for religous purposes; to prevent the excavation of sites of historic interest by ignorant and unauthorised persons; to secure control over traffic in antiquities and to acquire ownership, where necessary and possible, of monuments and objects of archaeological and historical interest. The act invested the executive, for the first time, with sufficient legal authority with regard to monuments in private ownership and was destined to make a new era in the preservation of archaeological remains in the country.

The programme of conservation naturally received the greatest emphasis during the Curzon regime, and in pursuing it the Governor General was well served by the new Director General, who had assumed the reins of his office on 22 February 1902. The latter brought to bear on his task a scientific approach and an aesthetic understanding never encountered before in the history of Indian archacology. In his 'Note on the operations and future conduct of the Archaeological Survey' dated 6 April 1903 he mapped out the general lines to be followed in arresting the process of decay in ancient monuments. He pointed out that hypothetical restorations were unwarranted, unless they were essential to the stability of a building; that every original component of a structure should be preserved intact, and demolition and reconstruction should be undertaken only if the structure could not be otherwise maintained; that restoration of carved stone, carved wood or plaster moulding should be undertaken only if artisans were able to attain the excellence of the old and that in no case were mythological and other scenes to be re-carved. These principles were embodied in a Government Resolution on 7 July 1903 and dictated the pattern which the conservation operations were to follow ever since.

The achievements of the period in the field of conservation were so many that it is possible to mention only a few. The Agra Fort was cleared of its military barracks and the colonnades around the Diwan-i-Am courtyard restored. The Taj Mahal was expurgated of its modern accretions, and the ruined colonnades of its fore-courts were rebuilt. Extensive repairs were carried out in the Qutb complex of buildings, the Mughal gardens in the historic forts of Shahjahan were restored to their pristine beauty, and the imperial palace buildings were given a new look by denuding them of all modern interpolations. The magnificent fabric of the sun temple at Konarak was salvaged from the deep accumulations of fallen stones and drifting sand in which it had been lying partly buried for centuries, and its wonderful plinth with its carved horses and chariot-wheels was again disclosed to the light of day. A vigorous campaign for conservation was similarly taken up and brought to successful completion at the magnificent mosque at Ajmer, at the Dilwara temples on Mt. Abu, at the tower of fame in Chitor, among the splendid group of monuments at Dhar and Mandu, among the ruins of Gaur and Pandua, at the Gol Gumbaz in Bijapur, and among a host of other monuments which had been fast slipping into decay and were crying for succour. It was indeed an amazing record of achievements.

If conservation was able to push ahead during the regime, exploration did not lag far behind. One of the principal reasons for which Marshall had been appointed was that he might introduce into India the scientific methods of digging which had yielded brilliant results in Greece and Crete, But Marshall felt, and his views were shared by Lord Curzon, that excavations, to start with, should be conducted on a limited scale to safeguard adequately against unscientific and reckless diggings. In his note on the conduct of archaeological survey already referred to Marshall pointed out: 'We shall endeavour to rescue any sites in danger of destructon and carry forward general exploration on a limited scale.... The many adverse criticisms levelled at Indian excavations in the past should make us doubly careful not to add to the examples of unscientific work.' Since 1898 there had been under the consideration of the Government a proposal mooted by the Eleventh Congress of Orientalists to form an Indian Exploration Fund which was to sponsor excavation of Indian sites by trained European experts. But Curzon promptly ruled it out. 'The last thing that we want', he observed, 'is the continental expert with a spade in hand. Let us excavate our own sites.'

The first excavation to be taken up by Marshall was that of Charsàda, the site of ancient Pushkalavati in which he had the collaboration of Dr. J.P. Vogel. This was one of the principal centres of Indo-Hellenistic civilisation and its selection opened up a new chapter in Indian archaeology by presaging the the pattern which archaeological explorations were to display during the first two decades of the century. This was followed by excavations in Sarnath, Kasia, and Rajgriha, at Basarh, the ancient Vaisali, and among the tumili at Lauriya Nandangarh, all associated with the history of Buddhism. But of far greater significance, from the point of view of its immediate effect and the amazing richness of its yields, was the expedition undertaken between 1900 and 1901 by Aurel (later Sir Aurel) Stein (pl. VIII) with the approval and support of Curzon's Government on the fringe of the Taklamakan desert, some sixty miles north of Niya. Here, following up the clues of native 'prospectors', Stein came upon the ruins of an ancient settlement abandoned sometime towards the end of the third century A.D. As he cleared room after room of sand Stein recovered just the kind of relics which an archaeologist needs for the reconstruction of the entire picture of a lost civilisation. He found wooden tablets bearing writings and tamarisk pens, wooden chop-sticks and spindles, a guitar with broken strings and broomsticks, rags of felt and woven fabrics and silk, to mention only a few items. Among the most important finds were a series of documents written in the Kharoshthi script vividly reflecting the intimate contact India once used to have with a region politically subject to China Stein's discovery also furnished the first tangible evidence of the spread of Buddhism from India to China, and opened up new possibilities for research on the till then obscure history of cultural and commercial contacts between India and Central Asia.

When in 1905 the archaeological survey became ripe for official review it could already point to a record of exceptionally brilliant achievements. By that date it had become sufficiently clear that the archaeological problems of a vast country like India were too complex and too gigantic to be successfully tackled within a short space of five years, and that the existing survey machinery required to be reorganised on a permanent basis if these problems were to be tackled at all. Marshall, in fact, had pleaded for the continuation of the Department as a permanent measure as early as 1904. 'I may refer at the outset,' he had argued in a note dated 19 April, 'to an illusory belief to which an expression had often been given that a time would soon come when the Archaeological Survey might be disbanded and the work of conservation, if not complete, accomplished through the agency of the Public Works Department. That time has receded further year by year, and the phantom might now, once for all, be laid to rest.'

Marshall's proposal received from Lord Curzon's Government their most enthusiastic support. Yet the problem relating to the future of the Survey was vigorously debated between Calcutta and London for well-nigh two years, and it was not until January 1906 that the Secretary of State saw light and became convinced that a permanent machinery to look after the archaeological interests of the country was a basic need, the fulfilment of which could no longer be delayed. His approval was communicated on 26 January 1906 to the Indian Government who followed it up by a resolution published on 28 April announcing that the Survey had been placed on a permanent and extended basis.

The seeds which Curzon had sown were about to sprout at last. But he had already relinquished the charge of his office. On his departure, Indian Archaeological Survey not only lost its sincerest friend and most effective champion but its actual founder. The responsibility of building progressively upon the foundation he had so carefully laid and of continuing unweakened the tradition he had so laboriously founded fell on the shoulders of the young Director General who had been his closest collaborator in all these labours of love.

THE MARSHALL EPOCH

THE twentythree years following Lord Curzon's departure, during which John Marshall was practically in the sole command in the archaeological field in India, form one of the most fascinating and fruitful epochs in the cultural annals of the country. The period witnessed the swift blossoming of the ideas which Curzon had bequeathed to posterity, the emergence, at an almost phenomenal speed, of a gigantic survey organisation on the foundation he had laid; and crowning all, a rapid succession of magnificent achievements, almost unparallelled, history in, in conservation, research and exploration. But it also witnessed something even of greater moment, to wit, a wholesale transformation in the very outlook of Indian archaeology.

Archaeology, before Marshall's time, had simply meant a quest for *objets d'art* or religious relics, a search for things which pleased the eye or satisfied a craving in the soul. But Marshall who had, while in Greece and Mycenae, imbibed the spirit of Schliemann and Dörpfeld, though perhaps not their techniques, intended from the very outset to make that science serve a purpose altogether different. He wanted it, first and foremost, to recapture the total culture of India in past ages, with their cities and streets, their furniture and tools, their arms and weapons, their ornaments and jewels, their seals and coins and their laws and customs. To this one end was keyed most of his exploration programmes, as would be amply evidenced by the number and the historical importance of the ancient sites laid bare during his regime,—Nalanda and Vaisali, Pataliputra and Bhita, three cities of Taxila and, crowning all, the protohistoric towns of Mohenjo-daro and Harappa. Not only did he conceive these and other programmes but with his master hand he worked out all the details, fixed and wrote down the methods, and sketched also the blue-prints for all future research. Great as were indeed the number and the magnitude of the discoveries which stand to his credit his title to fame rests no more on them than the new shape which he was able to give to the archaeological discipline itself. The period during which he guided the destiny of Indian archaeology was so deeply tinged by his colourful, dynamic and all-pervasive personality that even today he stands as the very symbol of that period, just as Cunningham impersonates for us an earlier age in archaeological history.

Yet, Marshall had to start literally from scratch, and, despite the patronage he had received during the initial stages of his career from an unusually enlightened Governor General, he had to go through fire and water to win for Indian archaeology its fundamental rights, its right not only to exist but to attain the highest pinnacle of self-realisation.

In the accomplishment of this colossal task Marshall, to begin with, was able to get the assistance of no more than half a dozen officers, Henry Cousens and Alexander Rea in Western and Southern Circles, Dr.T. Bloch in Bengal, Dr. Vogel in Panjab and Taw Sein Ko in Burma. In 1903 the strength of this small corps of workers was reinforced by the addition of an Architectural Surveyor in the United Provinces and an Assistant Superintendent, Dr. D.R. Bhandarkar in Bombay. But a real acquisition of the period was Sir Aurel Stein who combined the duties of Archaeological Superintendent in the North-West Frontier and Baluchistan with those of Inspector-General of Education. Marshall, however, endeavoured to fill the obvious gaps in the existing arrangement by enlisting, by offers of scholarship which were to be followed by suitable training, the assistance of Indian scholars interested in archaeological work. It was by these means he was able to attract to the service men like D.R. Sahni, K.N. Dikshit, and M.S. Vats, all of whom subsequently rose to the supreme position in the Survey.

As a result of the reform of 1906 the survey was strengthened by the arrival of Dr. Sten Konow, A.H. Longhurst and Dr. D.B. Spooner, all of them being scholars who were to bring distinction to the Department. But a set-back came in 1912 when an abortive attempt was made by the Government to decentralise the Survey by abolishing the post of the Director General and replacing it by a professor of Archaeology. The latter was to be attached to a proposed Oriental Research Institute. The move was backed by the argument that the survey was heavily in arrears in the matter of publication and that it had done nothing to attract Indian talent to archaeological work. It raised a storm of protest in India as well as abroad. The authorities in London found themselves unable to agree with the Government of India and the move completely fell through. It was ultimately decided to continue the Survey as it was, but in order to encourage Indian talent, two scholarships were created for the training of Sanskrit scholars in addition to those already existing since 1903. In 1917 the strength of the Survey was further reinforced by the appointment of an Archaeological Chemist, and in 1918 by that of an Assistant Director General, whose designation was changed to Deputy Director General in the following year.

The first world war had resulted in drastic reduction in the funds of the Survey leading to the suspension of a number of archaeological programmes. The peace which returned in 1918 was followed by a fresh series of changes affecting both the status and the organisation of the Department. The Devolution Rules of 1921 which came in the wake of the Montagu-Chelmsford Reforms of 1919 classified archaeology, for the first time, as a central subject. The immediate effect of this was to bring under the control of the centre all monuments that had been declared as protected under the Act of 1904, leaving the Local Governments to deal only with 'unprotected' monuments. The other consequence of the Reforms was to transform archaeological expenditure into a central charge, and although the administrative control of the archaeological staff in the different Circles was still left with the Local Governments that control was henceforth to be exercised by the latter only as agents of the Centre. The control in consequence tended to become formal and was in a few years' time totally abolished.

The year 1921 also witnessed a number of significant changes in the administrative structure of the Survey. The strength of the survey was reinforced by the creation of two additional Superintendents, one each for Epigraphy and the Archaeological section of the Indian Museum, two Assistant Superintendents for Epigraphy and two more Assistant Superintendents as reserve. This was also accompanied by a substantial all-round increase in salaries and by an assurance from the Government, embodied in their Resolution of 14 June 1921, that sixty per cent of the service might, henceforth, be filled only by Indians. The immediate effect of the reorganisation was to bring within the fold of the Survey three distinguished scholars, Hirananda Sastri, K.V. S. Aiyar, and R.P. Chanda. But within two years of the event there was another turn in the wheel of the Survey's fortune and the Inchcape Committee on Retrenchment dealt it a blow which seemed to imperil its very existence. The Committee proposed to reduce the Survey's funds by ninety per cent, stopping all exploration and even closing the famous Mughal gardens of Delhi, Agra, and Lahore. But fortunately for the Department both the Secretary of the State and the Viceroy threw their weight against the move and the Survey escaped the disaster with a cut of twenty-two and a half per cent.

Fortune once again began to smile on the Department and an endeavour was made in 1926 to create a permanent fund for archaeological exploration and thus to ensure for that object a secure yearly provision instead of the extremely uncertain and elusive budget voted by the Legislature. Though nothing came out of this effort, the grant for exploration was increased for the next two years to a sum of two lakh rupees and a half, and in 1926-27 four additional officers, a Deputy Director General and three Assistant Superintendents, were sanctioned to help exclusively in the work of exploration. The posts were put on a permanent basis two years later. These measures enabled Marshall to constitute a separate Exploration Branch to speed up the vast programme he had undertaken of exploring and excavating ancient sites. The Survey organisation was now complete. From a frail and tiny fabric it had grown into a massive and gigantic structure solidly built on a strong foundation. It had, in the words of one of his successors, 'become the largest and most complex archaeological machine in the world.'

This amazing transformation was possible because of the unparallelled devotion and industry, imagination and understanding which Marshall had brought to bear on the task of building up Indian archaeology. He had, in fact, given eloquent proofs of his insight into the archaeological problems of the country even from the day he had assumed the reins of his office, and his 'Note on the operations and future conduct of Archaeological Survey (6 April 1903), to which a reference has already been made, and which formed the basis of all his future programmes whether relating to preservation, exploration, epigraphy or maintenance of museums, shows unmistakably how comprehensive his approach was in respect to these subjects.

His initial reactions to the problems of conservation have already been noted and need not be referred to again. His ideas on the subject were given a mature shape in his note reviewing the archaeological progress in the country which was later embodied in a Government Resolution dated 22 October 1915 and published in a book form the next year. In this note Marshall pointed out the deplorable harm that could be done to ancient buildings in the name of restoration, and deprecated its being undertaken except in special circumstances. He, however, drew a distinction between the older Buddhist, Hindu and Jain edifices on the one hand and the more modern erections of the Muslims on the other. In the latter case he felt that a policy of limited restoration was sometimes not only desirable but justified on the ground that the art of the original builders was still a living art. He also held that in the case of monuments which were still serving the purpose for which they had been built, there were frequently valid reasons for restoring to more extensive measures of repair than would have been desirable, had the buildings been maintained merely as antiquarian relics. With these reservations demanded by the special conditions prevailing in India, the object which Marshall wanted to pursue was not to reproduce what had been defaced or destroyed. but to save what was left from further injury or decay and to preserve it as a national heir-loom or portents. These principles found concrete expression in a vast mulplicity of conservation programmes, which were undertaken and brought to a successful conclusion during his regime. It remains to add that these are the very principles which still govern the preservation activities of the Government of India.

Marshall showed an equally firm grasp of the problems relating to museum administration in India and in his programmes museums received a priority which was quite novel in their history. Even as early as 1903 he had recognised the need for close collaboration between the Survey over which he presided and the museums housing archaeological collections and had suggested the desirability of associating Archaeological Superintendents with the administration of the antiquarian sections in the Provincial museums in their respective circles. The suggestion, in the long run, bore fruit in the actual association of the members of the Survey with a number of leading museums. Thus, from 1906 to 1927, the Peshawar Museum had as its Honorary Curator the successive Superintendents of the Frontier Circle, and the archaeological section, Indian Museum at Calcutta had the service of a full-time Superintendent belonging to the archaeological service from 1921 onwards. Eleven years earlier, following the enactment of the Indian Museum Act, the Director General had become a trustee of the latter Museum.

Marshall was responsible for setting up a large number of museums under the direct control of the Survey including those at Agra, New Delhi, Delhi Fort, Lahore Fort, Mandalay, and the excavated sites of Taxila, Mohenjo-daro, Harappa, Sarnath, Nalanda and Pagan. The Museum at New Delhi was created to house, among other things, the antiquities collected by Sir Aurel Stein during his Central Asian expeditions of 1906-1908 and 1913-16. Once started, the muesum movement thrived rapidly and new museums came to be founded in rapid succession at Bijapur and Baripada, Chamba and Ajmer, Gwalior and Khajuraho, Sanchi and Dacca.

Epigraphical researches underwent a complete reorientation during the regime. As the Circle Officers usually had their hands too full with exploratory and conservation work to enable them to address themselves to epigraphical tasks, Marshall considered it desirable that these tasks should be exclusively entrusted to the Government Epigraphist who was also, by reason of his special command of the subject, was better qualified to do justice to it. He was able to place his scheme on a firmer basis when, following the reorganisation of 1906, he obtained a new post of Government Epigraphist serving the whole of India in lieu of an epigraphist concerned only with southern inscriptions. For Arabic and Persian inscriptions arrangement had been made as early as 1903 to start a separate journal, *Epigraphia Indo-Moslemica*, whose editing was entrusted, first, to Dr. (Later Sir) E. Denison Ross (1903-1908) and, later, to Dr. J. Horovitz (1909-12). On the latter's relinquishment of the charge Ghulam Yazdani, Director of Archaeology in Hyderabad (Deccan), became Government Epigraphist for Muslim inscriptions.

Among other achievements of Marshall in the organisational field may be mentioned his building up of an excellent reference library, since christened the Central Archaeological Library, which now contains more than 40,000 volumes and an equally rich photographic collection illustrating archaeological monuments and relics, which is one of the best in the country.

The regime also witnessed a thorough reorganisation in the publication programme of the Department. While *The New Imperial Series*, which had been started by Burgess in 1874, was continued, and arrangement was made for enriching it by further scholarly contribution, on a wide variety of archaeological topics, the gaps left in the arrangement in respect to the prompt recording of the Survey's own activities were amply remedied by the inauguration of a new series, the magnificent *Annual Reports of the Director General of Archaeology*, beautifully produced and sumptuously illustrated. Here the whole work of the Department was surveyed and described with well-written papers on conservation, exploration, epigraphy and museum-activities as also on archaeological operations undertaken in the Indian States. The *Reports*, which were continued till 1937, form a veritable mine of information on a vast range of problems relating to Indian archaeology and are indispensable to all students of history who have any hankering after India's past or any feeling for her ancient monuments. The series was supplemented in 1919 by yet another, the *Memoirs of the Archaeological Survey of India*, each volume in which was devoted to a special topic whether relating to exploration or excavation, study or conservation of monuments, epigraphical researches or any other field connected with the past relics of the country on which investigations had been completed or were in progress. Among other publishing ventures mention may be made of the revival of the well-known epigraphical series, *The Corpus Inscriptionum Indicarum*, in which two monumental *corpora* of epigraphs were completed during the period; a revised and enlarged edition of Asokan Inscriptions by Hultzsch (1925) and a volume of Kharoshthi inscriptions by Sten Konow (1929).

Equally noteworthy is the part which the Survey organisation played, under Marshall's leadership, in stimulating archaeological activities in the Indian States. Mysore, which had been maintaining an archaeological Department since 1890, undertook, on Marshall's suggestion a regular programme of exploration and architectural survey, yielding as a result, a rich harvest of epigraphical and antiquarian publications. In 1924 the State passed an Ancient Monuments Preservation Regulation, thereby providing its immortal archaeological relics with the protection which had been their crying need for ages. The example of Mysore was followed by other states. Travancore appointed its first Superintendent of Archaeology in 1908. Kashmir constituted an archaeological department in 1912, Gwalior in 1913 and Hyderabad in 1914. All these States, and many others, readily extended their cooperation to the central organisation in the accomplishment of the great mission which the latter had taken up of salvaging the lost pages of the country's history. Mysore's publishing enterprises were emulated in other States. Among the most significant of these particularly deserving of mention is the project undertaken by Hyderabad to reproduce the Ajanta frescoes by photographic process, in order to keep for posterity an authentic record of this priceless heritage of Indian art. The State also spent liberally on the conservation not only of these frescoes but of other important monuments within its jurisdiction. To the States which did not have any archaeological organisation of their own, substantial help, both technical and financial was often extended by the Centre. The excavation and conservation works at Sanchi, for instance, were carried out under Marshall's personal supervision, and the Dhar and Chhatarpur States were liberally helped in the salvaging of the splendid complex of edifices adorning respectively Mandu and Khajuraho and comprising some of the noblest examples of monumental architecture in India.

All these constitute an astonishing record. Yet they are completely thrown into the shade by the much greater achievements of the period in the field of survey and exploration. Indeed the projects which were under taken or accomplished in this field by Marshall and his colleagues were so colossal both in their scale and in their number and so amazing from the point of view of the complexity, richness and far-reaching effects of their yields that it is possible here to do no more than refer to the general trends which characterised them. The Survey's attention was at first directed to the well-known Buddhist sites like Sarnath and Kasia, Sravasti and Rajgir, Vaisali and Sanchi, Takht-i-Bahi and Shahji-ki-Dheri to mention only a few. The reason of this was that the survey at this time was better informed—thanks to the Chinese pilgrims and the researches of earlier archaeologists—about these sites generally than about any other class of remains, and it seemed to Marshall 'safer to start with these and make some of our ground before groping our way further into the unknown'. Marshall had also another reason for his preference. He believed that he was 'more likely to get spectacular finds on these Buddhist sites than anywhere else, and such finds were absolutely indispensable to us, if we were to interest the public in our work and secure more adequate funds for it'.

Subsequent events more than vindicated the policy. Most of the sites attached came to yield an extremely rich harvest of monuments, sculptures, reliquary and other antiquities which captured at once popular imagination, thus making infinitely easy the task of extending enquiries to other fields of archaeology, which in Marshall's view would not otherwise have been possible. From Sarnath were obtained an exceptionally rich crop of stone sculptures including the famous lion capital , a colossal Bodhisattva image of the reign of Kanishka and a huge hoard of Buddhist images dating from the Gupta age. Sravasti likewise yielded, in addition to ruined houses, a number of brick-built stupas and shrines, in the debris of one of which was discovered a group of more than three hundred terra-cottas of the Gupta age depicting scenes from the Rama-yana. The excavations carried out at Sanchi brought for the first time to view no less than fifty-one edifices till then hidden under debris. At Nalanda the efforts of the survey resulted in the exploration of a vast complex of religious buildings, occupying an area more than 2000 feet in length and 700 feet in width, and consisting of harmoniously planned rows of stupas, chaityas and monasteries. At Shahji-ki-Dheri were discovered the remains of the famous stupa of Kanish-ka which yielded, among other treasures, a relic casket of guilt bronze beautifully decorated with seated Buddhas, garland carriers and geese, and displaying a harmonious blending of Indian and Hellenistic artmotifs. Equally rewarding were the excavations carried out among the complex of buildings comprised in the Bud-dhist settlements near Taxila, particularly at the Dharma-rajika stupa and at Jaulian (pl. XL) from each of which were recovered a splendid array of sculptures and anti quities. These excavations give a singularly lucid picture of a new type of Buddhist establishment which was developed in the northwest and which consisted initial-ly of an open air stupa of imposing dimensions with a variety of detached buildings surrounding it. All these constitute no more than an illustrative list. Even so they will serve as a fairly accurate index to the great volume of work which was accomplished during the period.

Marshall, however, felt equally exercised about the value of ancient city-sites where he naturally expected discoveries of a more illuminating order. Among the sites first to receive his attention may be mentioned Bhita, where the excavations carried out by the Survey partially exposed a mercantile settlement and brought to light, in addition to a number of tribal and Kushan coins, terracotta figurines and plaques, (pl. XXXIX) an interesting hoard of sealings, many of them of mercantile origin, which testify to a thriving trade from which the city at one time used to draw its nourishment. Hardly less significant were the diggings made in Kumrahar and Bulandibagh, near Patna. From the first site were recovered the remnants of a pillared hall belonging, to all appearance, to the Maurya palace at ancient Pataliputra, and from the second the fragments of what has been identified as the wooden palisade of the same city, mentioned in glowing terms by Megasthenes and the classical writers who echoed him.

It was, however, at Taxila where Marshall's campaign extended to more than twenty years, that he was able to obtain the most comprehensive and instructive results, revolutionising thereby our entire conception of urban life in north-west India from the seventh century B.C. to the fifth century A.D. Here he was able to expose to view three successive cities of greatest importance , the first, recovered from the Bhir Mound, which dated from pre-Alexandrian times and presented typically Indian features, the second, located at Sirkap, which was founded by the Bactrian Greeks following the true Hippodamian plan with straight streets cutting each other at right angles and dividing up the city into rectangular blocks, and rebuilt on the same plan but on a more improved basis by the Indo-Parthians (pl. XLI), and the third, the town of the Kushans, which was discovered at Sirsukh.

The importance of the first site arises from the fact that it affords a vivid glimpse into the urban way of life as in vogue in north-west India from pre-Alexandrian times to the end of the Maurya era, bringing at the same time to light the nature and extent of Indo-Hellenistic contacts during the period. The site also yielded a rich crop of 'minor' antiquities including a new type of lustrous pottery, which although its significance could not be grasped at the moment, was destined, under the appellation given it later of Northern Black Polished Ware, to symbolise a very important and widely distributed culture-complex whose centres of dispersion have since been located in the Ganga plain. Of more immediate significance was the site of the Parthian town at Sirkap, which was subjected to extensive excavations, with a view to bringing to complete view the entire layout of the town. Although Marshall has sometimes been criticised for not having resorted to vertical digging which alone could give us valuable stratigraphic information about the site, it is all the same doubtful if he could have, in that case, given the picture we owe to him of a teeming city with its streets and its temples and its palaces and its shops. It would seem that following a technique that was perhaps wrong he had arrived at a result which was extremely desirable.

While ancient Buddhist and Graeco-Indian sites were thus being attacked by Marshall and his colleagues steps were taken to despatch exploratory missions to India's borderlands and beyond with a view to unravelling the history of India's contacts with not only with Centra

Asia but also with territories culturally affiliated to Tibet and China As early as 1900 Sir Aurel Stein had undertaken an expedition to Niya on the fringe of the Taklamakan and had unearthed a most interesting buried settlement there. He led another expedition in the same direction in 1906-1908 in the course of which he made a re-examination of the Niya oasis, and gathered a rich harvest of Kharoshthi documents. After visiting Loulan and Miran and a number of important sites, he finally reached the famous 'Halls of Thousand Buddhas 'at Tun-huang which yielded him an amazing crop of antiquities, including, among others, a unique collection of documents in the Brahmi script bearing texts not only in Khotanese and Tokharian, but in Sanskrit as well. The harvest also included a marvellous array of paintings on silk, cotton and paper, depicting legendary scenes from Buddhas' life and other Buddhistic themes and displaying unmistakable imprints of Graeco-Buddhistic influences. Yet another expedition was conducted by Stein in 1913-16, which enabled him to recover a large collection of wall-paintings from Miran, to re-explore Tun-huang which yielded a fresh, rcrop of archaeological finds equally rich, and, finally to attempt the clearance of an extensive burial ground in Turfan, from which he was able to recover, among others, a rich collection of fine figured silks and other decorated fabrics with which the entombed dead bodies found there had been wrapped. Only a very brief reference is possible to the magnificent discoveries which Stein was able to make in the course of his expeditions. The details are fully recorded in the eleven quarto volumes of *Ancient Khotan* (1907), *Serindia* (1921), *Innermost Asia* (1928), all being from his scholarly pen.

Splendid as were these discoveries they form a fitting prelude to other and more astounding discoveries which were awaiting archaeologists within the Indian territory. In 1921 Daya Ram Sahni, while excavating three of the mounds of Harappa, unearthed, besides other antiquities, two pictographic seals similar to the one which had already been noticed by Cunningham fifty-two years earlier. Though the prehistoric nature of the site was established, its age could not be determined at the moment. But about the same time came the astounding discoveries made by R.D. Banerji while he was cutting through a mound at Mohenjo-daro in Sind (pl. XLII), four hundred miles away. In the course of his operations Banerji reached levels yielding seals exactly like those at Harappa and at once recognised their prehistoric character. Though his attempt to connect them with Minoan antiquities proved abortive his guess that they might be dated in the second or the third millennium B.C. wasnot far wide of the mark.

In 1924 the antiquities from both these sites were examined by Marshall who came instantly to the conclusion that they belonged 'to the same stage of culture and approximately to the same age and that they were distinct from anything previously known to us in India'. This was followed by an article he contributed to the *Illustrated London News* (20 September) announcing the discoveries and comparing them, quite justifiedly, with Schliemann's at Tiryns and Mycenae, an announcement which took the world of archaeologists literally by storm. Professor Sayce immediately rushed to the press to point out the resemblance he had come to detect between the antiquities from the Indus Valley and certain Sumerian objects from south Iraq, while C.J. Gadd and

Sidney Smith made a conjoined effort to trace the affinities between Indian and Babylonian relics, thereby furnishing a rough basis for establishing a synchronism between the new civilisation and Dynastic Sumer, then referable approximately to the beginning of the third millennium B.C. or even a little earlier. The synchronism was later confirmed by the actual discovery of Indian seals or seals of Indian inspiration in Sumerian sites both in Early dynastic and Akkadian contexts. Thus almost with dramatic suddenness the Indian archaeologist found himself on an equal footing with his colleagues in the Mesopotamian and the Nile Valleys. 'At a single bound', said Marshall, 'we have taken back our knowledge of Indian civilisation some 3000 years earlier and have established the fact that in the third millennium before Christ, or even before that, the peoples of the Panjab and Sind were living in well-built cities and were in possession of a relatively mature culture with a high standard of art and crafts manship and a developed system of pictographicwriting.'

The discoveries encouraged Marshall to organise further exploration of the two sites. The excavations at Mohenjo-daro were resumed by Vats, who lay bare several distinct occupation levels lying one above another. The work was continued by Dikshit in 1924-25, and in 1925-26 more extensive excavations were carried out by Marshall himself in collaboration with Hargreaves, Dikshit and E.J.H. Mackay, in 1926 by Sahni and and Mackay, and in 1927-31 by Mackay alone. The results of the 1921-27 excavations were embodied in Marshall's three monumental volumes, *Mohenjo-daro and the Indus Civilisation* (London 1931) and Mackay published the results of his work in *Further Excavations at Mohenjo-daro* (Delhi 1938). At Harappa, Sahni continued to explore from 1923-25 and thereafter the task was taken up by Vats.

All these activities brought to light a highly sophisticated bronze age civilisation, symbolised by densely populated cities carefully planned with harmonious rows of burnt brick houses and streets crossing each other at right angles and elaborately furnished with wells, drains, bathrooms and other sanitary arrangements, by highly skilled industries which were organised, standardised and controlled centrally, by a far-flung commerce probably equally under the control of a central authority, by a unique pottery painted with black design on red-slips and, finally, by a pictographic script, the use of which was probably limited to the ruling minority. The civilisation did not seem to posses any public art. The only art it knew of was represented by pottery designs, engraved seals, clay and terracotta figurines and some sculptures in the round of a remarkably high standard. Although tools of bronze, copper and stone were in use in both the cities there was no evidence of any multiplication of war-weapons attesting internecine strifes as in the case of the Mesopotamian city-states.

Simultaneously with the excavations which were going on in both the cities an endeavour was made to locate traces of the newly discovered civilisation in other parts of the country as well. In 1925-26 Hargreaves laid bare a site representing a chalcolithic culture characterised by an unusual type of polychrome pottery and two different kinds of burial, complete and fractional. In 1925 Dikshit came across two new sites of the Harappa civilisation: Lohumjo-daro in Larkana and

Limujunejo in upper Sind. In 1926 N.G. Majumdar conducted a trial excavation at Jhukar which yielded two levels of a culture akin to the Harappan and yet another overlying it which was characterised by a buff ware with black and red decoration and stone and clay stamp-seals, and was definitely post-Harappan. Between 1926 and 1928 Sir Aurel Stein made a survey of Baluchistan and located a number of chalcolithic sites representing different stages of development, some of which were pre-Harappan in character, while others yielded cultures overlapping or post-dating them. Among important sites discovered were Rana Ghundai, Periano Ghundai, Kulli, Mehi, Nundara Sukhtagendor and Shahi Tump. These reconnaisances not only effected a radical expansion in the existing knowledge of the nature and extent of protohistoric cultures in the north and northwest of the Indian sub-continent but posed a host of new problems which the archaeologist was now called upon to tackle.

In the midst of these activities Sir John Marshall relinquished the charge of his office on 6 September 1928. He was placed on special duty for supervising and directing the operations at Taxila and for coordinating the results of the explorations in the Indus Valley sites and other sites allied to them. He was also to write a series of monographs on the important excavated sites. On 19 March 1931 he was due for retirement, but his service was retained till 15th March 1934, when he finally left for England. Of the monograph he undertook to write reference has already been made to his monumental *Mohenjo-daro and the Indus Civilisation*. Others are : *Monuments of Sanchi*, 2 volumes (Delhi, 1940): *Taxila*, 3 volumes (Cambridge, 1951).

It is not easy to over-estimate the services rendered by Marshall to the cause of Indian archaeology. The problem which confronted him were as numerous as they were formidable, and it stands to his credit that he attacked most of them bravely and with success, and was able, in the end, to build up what proved to be, and still is, the biggest and most complex apparatus for archaeological investigations in the world. That apparatus has undergone very little change since his time and despite the many vicissitudes through which the Department has had to pass after he left the scope which he defined for it by laying equal emphasis on the four branches of its activities, conservation, exploration, epigraphy and museum administration, remains fundamentally the same.

The charge has recently been laid at Sir John Marshall's door that he committed a grave error in archaeological strategy by concentrating on one class of sites to the exclusion of all others thus preventing a comprehensive index being compiled to the cultures of all the different ages in India. Thus, till 1921 he directed his attention only to the Buddhist and Indo-Greek monuments and later, after the epoch-making discoveries at Mohenjo-daro and Harappa, almost exclusively to the chalcolithic sites in the northwest. Yet it is easy to see why Marshall behaved in the way he did. The major problem before him was how to kindle the interest of the general publicin the investigations the Archaeological Survey was pursuing, and nothing short of spectacular discoveries, such as were made, for instance, at Nalanda and Sanchi, Sarnath and Taxila, Mohenjo-daro and Harappa, would have, as Marshall rightly felt, made .people visualise the wonders which the archaeologist's spade could unravel

As Marshall himself admits, 'in the course of twenty years of digging at Taxila, I found it advisable to be frequently varying my programme, at one time occupying myself with Buddhist monasteries scattered over the countryside, at another with one or other of the city sites; for although the latter were archaeologically more important, it was the monasteries with their wealth of sculptures........that helped to keep alive public interest. His strategy, moreover, was justified by its success. The epoch-making discoveries he made enabled him not only to save his Department from impending ruin when the axe of the Inchcape Committee was about to fall on it in 1923 but to obtain from the Government liberal grants for excavation.

A more serious criticism of Marshall is that the methods used by him in the excavation of sites were not always free from fault, that he ignored natural stratification and depended mostly on artificial levelling in fixing the inter-relations of the different phases of an excavated site, and that in making a clearance he often unwittingly destroyed the very evidence which it was necessary for him to record. This charge may be largely true but that should not justify our ignoring the fact that Marshall's standards, despite their obvious shortcomings, were not much behind those of many of his colleagues in the near east, and that even a giant like Sir Flinders Petrie, whose contribution to the science of archaeology was greater than any single man's in his own days, has not been able to escape the gibes of modern criticism. But faulty as were Marshall's methods he yet found it possible often to arrive at a correct or near-correct result when pursuing an investigation. All criticisms become silenced when one turns one's eyes to two of his masterly archaeological epics—Parthian Taxila and protohistoric Mohenjo-daro. In both cases he was able, as though with a conjurer's wand, to re-create a whole phase of human society teeming with life. Yet in both cases he achieved his aim despite the defects in his methods. And *pace* all his critics Marshall will always be remembered as the man, who archaeologically speaking, left India three thousand years older than he had found her.

AFTER JOHN MARSHALL

THE mantle of Marshall fell on an enthusiastic band of archaeologists who had been closely associated with him in all his work and had assimilated his teachings as well as methods of work. The band includes such distinguished names as H. Hargreaves, Daya Ram Sahni, K.N. Dikshit, N.G. Majumdar and M.S. Vats, all of them men of great ability who had specialised in their respective fields of work. On these men now devolved the task of continuing the tradition which Marshall had so laboriously built up and of upholding the cause of archaeology in India.

The first to receive the call to fill the gap left by Marshall's retirement was Hargreaves, who held the charge of the Director General from 8 October 1928 to 29 July, 1931. He was succeeded in the office by Rai Bahadur Daya Ram Sahni the first Indian to rise to the supreme position in the Archaeological Survey of India. On Śahni's retirement the office devolved on J.F. Blakiston on 1 June 1935, who after a short tenure of less than two years handed over the charge to Rao Bahadur K.N. Dikshit on 21 March 1937. Dikshit remained at the helm of affairs for a relatively long perod of seven years, retiring in 1944 (pl. IX).

This entire period extending to about sixteen years was rendered memorable by the heroic efforts made by Marshall's immediate successors to maintain intact the system he had bequeathed and to complete the tasks which he had left unfinished. In these efforts they were largely successful even though they had to wrestle with many an obstacle almost at every step, thanks specially to the extremely unimaginative and indifferent attitude which the Government of the day chose to adopt towards archaeological work. On the Survey again fell the axe of retrenchment in 1931. The number of its superior officers, as a consequence, was reduced from twentynine to twenty, the Exploration Branch was abolished, a large number of subordinate posts were done away with, scholarships were curtailed and funds for normal work underwent drastic reduction. The situation was further aggravated with the outbreak of the Second World War. The Government decided that no new monuments should be brought under protection for the duration of the war and that the publication work should be entirely stopped. Severe as these blows were they had a stunning effect on the Department, and it came almost to the verge of a break-down. If it succeeded in averting a complete wreck and in resuming its voyage towards its destined goal the credit is entirely due to the succession of able skippers to whom it had fallen to pilot it through this time of troubles.

The period witnessed a number of significant changes affecting both the administrative structure of the Department and the organisation of archaeological work in the country. In 1931 steps were taken to replace the post of Superintendent for Hindu and Buddhist monuments at Lahore by that of an Assistant Superintendent attached to the Frontier Circle and to re-designate the Superintendent for Muhammadan and British Monuments as Superintendent, Northern Circle. Thus a long-standing, cumbrous distinction, having no more than a denominational origin was done way with, and the activities of both the Circles were reorganised strictly on a regional basis. Further changes came in 1935 following the constitutional changes brought about by the Government of India Act of that year. The Burma circle was detached from the Survey and its activities were reorganised on an independent basis. Sind was separated from Bombay and added to the Frontier Circle. 'Ancient and historical monuments', including 'archaeological sites and remains' were made exclusively a federal subject with the result that in 1937 the Central Government were able to take over all powers till then vested in the Provinces under the Ancient Monuments Preservation Act in respect to the care and protection of ancient monuments and relics.

Of more immediate significance were the steps which were taken during the period to afford fresh impetus to archaeological explorations and excavations. In 1932 an amendment was effected in the section dealing with excavation in the Ancient Monuments Preservation Act so as to enable interested institutions and organisations, including foreign missions, to undertake excavations in protected sites subject to certain rules and conditions, which were framed by Government in this behalf. The first institutions to take advantage of the concession were the American School of Indic and Iranian Studies and the Boston Museum of Fine Arts, which jointly sent out a mission to India in 1935 to carry out excavations in the Chanhu-daro area in Sind, which led to most interesting results.

Endeavours were made during the regime of K.N. Dikshit to follow this up by encouraging Indian Universities and Institutions to participate in exploration work. For Dikshit very rightly believed that an indispensable condition for the advancement of the study of India's unknown past was the widespread extension of archaeological researches from the confines of a mere official organisation into the academic activities of the Universities and learned societies, from the monopoly, so to say, of the civil servant to the free initiative of the educated public. These efforts yielded its first fruits when the University of Calcutta took a license for excavating the ancient site of Bangarh in Dinajpur district, thus distinguishing itself as the first Indian University to actively participate in excavation. Dikshit also endeavoured to multiply the contacts of his Department not only with the Provincial Museums, but also with archaeological departments in the Indian States.

These distinctive achievements in organisation were more than matched by still greater achievements of the Survey in the field of exploration and excavation. While historical sites continued to receive attention as before, and many of them, like that at Paharpur (pl. XLIV), were subjected to extensive excavation, the Survey's energies were mainly directed towards the remains representing protohistoric cultures. Between 1929 and 1931 N. G. Majumdar discovered many new sites in Sind such as Chanhu-daro, Ali Murad, Amri, Lohri, Pandi Wahi. The first two sites yielded pottery identical with Harappan, while at the last three were found beneath the Harappa levels evidences of a culture which was characterised by a buff ceramic with black painted ornament and the frequent use of red in zones or lines and with no objects of metal except copper beads. The excavations at Harappa were continued by Vats till 1931 leading, among others, to two outstanding discoveries : structures characterised by parallel walls which were later identified as the Harappan granary area (pl. XLIII); and a cemetery, since designated cemetery H showing two distinct strata. In the lower stratum were found complete burials in which skeletons were accompanied by groups of pottery vessels, while the upper revealed a plethora of fractional burials in urns. The two strata were distinctly post-Harappan and represented an intrusive culture not exemplified elsewhere. The results of these excavations were published in *Excavations at Harappa* (Delhi 1940).

In 1929-30 Vats discovered a site at Rupar where pottery, terracotta, and other antiquities were unearthed closely resembling those from Harappa. In 1935 he discovered a similar site at a mound in Rangpur, which yielded a rich crop of objects distinctive of the Indus Valley civilisation. The area of the distribution of the civilisation was thus found as extending from south Baluchistan to northeast Punjab and from north Baluchistan to Kathiawar, an area immensely larger than those occupied by the chalcolithic civilisations of either Egypt or Sumeria. To pursue further enquiries in respect to the dispersion of chalcolithic cultures in India an expedition was organised in 1938 to carry out further exploration in Sind. While on duty, the leader of the expedition, Majumdar (pl. X) met with a tragic endat the hands of robbers. His death was a grievous blow to the cause of archaeology in India.

The period also witnessed a great revival of interest in the prehistoric stone age cultures in India. In 1930 M.C. Burkitt studied the collection of paleoliths made from the Krishna basin in South India by L.A. Cammiade, discovered a chronological sequence of types comparable with that recognised in Africa, and analysed the tools into the accepted framework of paleolithic epochal nomenclature. Three years later Helmut De Terra led the Yale-Cambridge North Indian Expedition, consisting of himself, Teilhard de Chardin and T.T. Paterson, to attack the problem of the Indian stone age in Kashmir and Panjab. In the course of his investigations De Terra found a characteristic industry with pebble choppers, and flakes and cores, to which he gave the name Sohan after the type site where the first specimens of the industry had been noticed. De Terra also distinguished pre-Sohan flakes in several respects similar to the products of the well-known Clactonian industry. There were thus discovered in India two distinct manufacturing traditions dating from the middle and upper pleistocene times, the first, the Sohan pebble chopper tradition of the north and the second, the hand axe tradition of the south. These discoveries played an effective role in changing the entire outlook of the Archaeological Survey itself towards Indian prehistory. The first outcome of the change was seen in the prehistoric expedition organised by K.N. Dikshit to the Sabarmati valley of Gujarat. This was, in the course of time, followed by other expeditions planned by the Archaeological Survey as well as other organisations.

All these make what may be regarded by any reasonable standard a distinguished record. Yet in 1939 the Department's activities came in for a lashing criticism from one of the leading European archaeologists, Sir Leonard Woolley. As early as 1938 there had been a talk of inviting a foreign expert to give Indian archaeologists the benefits of his advice. The proposal had met with enthusiastic response from K.N. Dikshit, whose view was that the expert should actually train up some of the members of the Survey in the up-to-date methods of excavation. The Government, however, acted differently, and Woolley, on whom their choice had fallen, was required to make only a review of the entire archaeological work in the country and to give his suggestions on future plan of work. He was to advise, among other matters, on the best methods and agencies for achieving the fruitful development of exploration activities in general, on the most promising sites or areas for excavations and also on any general point touching excavation or exploration.

These rather unusual terms of reference obliged Woolley to make a rapid tour, limited to barely three months, of all the important sites (forty-five in number) in India, both excavated and unexcavated, which he could think of and to arrive at a series of sweeping conclusions, a large part of which had their origin in a hurried observation of the sites and an insufficient understanding of the conditions prevailing. What he attempted in his report, which was submitted on 11 February 1939, was nothing short of a wholesale condemnation of the Archaeological Survey, much of which seems to be totally unjustified. He was right perhaps in criticising the existing policy of dispensing the funds available for excavation into small grants for work on a multiplicity of sites and the apparent indifference which was shown to 'the establishment of a typological sequence of antiquities.' He was perhaps equally right in advocating a better and more comprehensive planning that would take into consideration different classes of sites spread over all the country so that the archaeological gaps between the different cultures till then discovered could steadily be closed up. He was justified also in deprecating the existing tendency not to excavate sites to their lowest levels, which alone could reveal their full stratigraphic history, and in laying emphasis on the need for specialised training. But it is questionable if he was correct in totally condemning the Department's effort to conserve excavated remains, for example, at sites like Taxila and Mohenjo-Daro. His criticism of the methods followed by the Department in excavation is couched in extremely vague and general terms, and it is doubtful if he had time to detect what had really been at fault. He did not seem to know, for instance, that the excavators had been consistently using artificial levelling in determining the stratigraphical history of the sites excavated. It is also an equally debatable point if Woolley was right in advising the discontinuance of the work at Mohenjo-daro on the sole ground that the site was poor in painted pottery. What sensational facts relating to the site subsequent explorations were able to bring to light belong to more recent history and are too well known to require any expatiation here. There were many gaps in the archaeological work in the country, but the Archaeological Survey was not responsible for all of them, and one is not quite sure if while emphasising some of them the Woolley Report had taken into consideration all the facts relevant to the problem.

On the positive side the recommendations of Woolley included the appointment of an Adviser on Archaeology who was to deal with all the important issues involved in the Indian Archaeological field, and of two specialists in stone-age antiquities, 'proto-historians' as he called them. Another fruitful suggestion was that non-official institutions both foreign and Indian should be encouraged to take part in excavation work. Yet another positive feature of the Report was the emphasis it laid on the need for thoroughly excavating a select number of representative historical sites. Woolley himself had prepared a list of such sites, prominently figuring among which was Ahichchhatra (Ramnagar) in the district of Bareli.

The Woolley report as a whole was for the time being put on the shelf. But it was decided to implement immediately the recommendations relating to the excavation of Ahichchhatra. A large scale excavation of the site was accordingly undertaken during 1940–44 under the direction of Dikshit, in which special attention was directed to the typological classification of the ceramic finds, which ranged over about fifteen centuries. The resultant study provided Indian archaeology with a useful framework of reference against which subsequent ceramic finds could be tested. The excavation was also memorable for the discovery, to which it led, of further specimens of the so-called Northern Black Polished Ware, to which a reference has already been made, and of an entirely new ceramic type of fine grained clay with grey core painted with black or brown lines, which were recovered from the lowest levels and were later christened Painted Grey Ware (pl. XLV). The two types of pottery later came to symbolise two distinct culture-complexes with a wide range of dinstribution, the advent of the first being roughly assigned to the sixth or the fifth century B.C. and of the second to the beginning of the first millennium B.C.

K.N. Dikshit's retirement in 1944 marked the end of the era which had begun with Marshall and a new era was ushered in by the arrival on the scene of Brigadier (later Sir) R.E. Mortimer Wheeler, an eminent British Archaeologist, who was recalled from war-service to assume the charge of the Department. The period of his brief stewardship, which did not extend beyond the four year term of his contract, was one of the most eventful in the annals of Indian archaeology, and was marked by a series of significant changes not only in the organisation and the general planning of archaeological work but in the very tactics followed in the conduct of investigations.

Wheeler brought to his task the scientific methods of archaeological excavations which he had developed in England in the twenties and thirties from the earlier techniques among others, of Major Pitt-Rivers, reflected in the latter's excavations at Cranborne Chase, as also the administrative genius which he had shown as Director of National Museum of Wales and the London Museum. He believed that the excavation of a site, like the ordering of a battle, must be 'thought out and coordinated by a single present and directing mind' if chaos, waste and inefficiency were to be avoided. One of his first tasks on his arrival was to set up an Excavations Branch as a specialised nucleus of field-archaeology under an Assistant Superintendent (soon raised to the status of a Superintendent). This was followed by the creation of a number of other important posts, viz., that of a prehistorian, an Assistant Archaeological

Chemist, an Assistant Superintendent of Muslim Epigraphy in 1945 and a Superintendent of Publications in 1946.

Conservation received equal attention from the new Director General who, with a view to having a greater hold on all the archaeological remains and to maintaining a high standard of repair work, took steps to bring the entire conservation programme for the country under the direct control of the Survey. This led to the reorganisation of the administrative structure of each circle on a uniform basis with a Superintendent at the head of each, supported by a requisite staff, and the creation of an Executive Engineer at headquarters to meet the consequential increase in the Survey's responsibilities. To rationalise the distribution of duties among the different Circles a new South Eastern Circle was set up in 1947 to take charge of the Archaeological work of the Andhra districts of Madras, the whole of Orissa and a few areas of the Central Provinces.

The development of museums was given a high priority in Wheeler's scheme of reorganisation. In 1945 a Museums Branch was constituted under an Assistant Superintendent to look after the museum under the Survey's control, and in 1947 an Assistant Archaeological Chemist was created to reinforce the Museum personnel. Wheeler also took the initative in inducing the Government to set up a Committee to report on the functions, the purpose and the administrative organisation of a National Museum for India, and after the Committee, which was presided over by Sir Maurice Gwyer, had produced its report he made an all-out effort to ensure that its implementation was not inordinately delayed.

Wheeler placed equal emphasis on training in the different branches of archaeology. Conservation-courses were organised under his direction both for the members of the Department and for interested outsiders. Provision was also made for short-time training courses for students from Universities and other institutions in the techniques of excavation, preparation of field records, surveying, photography and administration, the object being to give the trainees a general idea of the standards aimed at by modern archaeological technique. Wheeler also felt that if Indian archaeology was to avoid being caught up again in stagnancy it should continue to maintain active contacts with the latest developments in the science in the progressive countries outside India, and chalked out a scheme of regular deputation abroad of the members of the Survey.

Yet another achievement of Wheeler was the inauguration of *Ancient India*, the bulletin of the Department, which, to quote his own words, was a venture 'to put archaeology regularly on to the book stalls, and to interest the educated Indian public in the current work relating to the exploration and conservation of the heritages of material culture'. A further innovation of the regime was the formation of a Central Advisory Board of Archaeology, which came into existence primarily through Wheeler's initiative. The object of the Board was to review 'the needs of archaeology in India—current and future' and to advise the Government on them as also 'to act as an intermediary between the Archaeological services, the world of learning administration and in some, small degree, the wider public'. It was composed of representatives of the Universities, learned societies, the Government and the Indian States. The Board has since its inception been rendering a useful service to the cause of archaeology in India.

In all these activities Wheeler had as his intimate collaborator Dr. N. P. Chakravarti, the eminent epigraphist who became Joint Director General towards the close of 1945. All that the former was able to achieve, to quote him again, 'would have been impossible but for the wise and devoted services' of his scholarly coadjutor.

The tremendous changes effected in the organisation of the Survey were but a prelude to the astonishing progress Wheeler was able to achieve in filling in the gaps in the existing archaeological evidence. The first task which he took up was that of re-studying the Indus cities with a view to ascertaining their true sociological character. Since Marshall it has been customary to regard the two cities as unique in the ancient east, peaceful mercantile communities having no experience of military autocracy or citadel rule such as characterised the political systems, for example, of contemporary Egypt and Mesopotamia. But a preliminary inspection of the highest mound at Harappa in May 1944 enabled Wheeler to discover the remains of what once had been the towers and battlements of a formidable acropolis 'defiantly feudal in aspect'. A subsequent inspection of the stupa mound at Mohenjo-daro brought to light a flood-worn remnants of a citadal of similar size and orientation to that of Harappa. Thus was exploded the prevailing idea of the non-military character of the Indus cities. Wheeler followed this up two years later by extensive excavations carried out at Harappa, in the course of which he was not only able to get confirmation of his preliminary observations but to discover certain new features about the life of the ancient city till then unknown—e.g., the widely prevailing practiceof extended burial (pl. XLVII).

Wheeler also suceeded in establishing for the first time accurate stratigraphic relationship between Harappan levels and the Cemetery H which was now conclusively attributed to a positively intrusive culture. But Wheeler's tentative proposal to associate this culture with the Aryan invaders and to make them responsible for the extinction of the Harappa civilisation has not found general acceptance. Be it added, however, that Wheeler himself did not view his theory as anything beyond a mere possibility. For a positive solution of the problem he looked forward to further explorations and diggings at other suitable sites.

The second problem which exercised Wheeler was that relating to the archaeology of south India. Here reliable written records were available continuously only from the 6th century A.D. Though material was abundant for earlier periods, its inter-relationship was unknown. But Wheeler realised that a potential datum line was provided by the impact of Roman commerce on central and southern India, with the consequent deposition of Roman coins and coin hoards of known dates. A suitable site was, therefore, needed which would afford the means for correlating the Roman with Indian materials. That site was ultimately found in Arikamedu, near Pondicherry, where Wheeler discovered an Indo-Roman trading station. The site yielded along with Indian materials several objects of import such as, for instance, sherds of the celebrated Italian red glazed pottery bearing the stamps among others, of the Vibii family of Arrezzo, and dating from the times of Augustus (pl. XLVI). An equation was at last found between dated imports and an indigenous culture, which Wheeler now proceeded to apply to the excavations carried out under his direction at the megalithicsite in Brahamagiri (pl. XLVIII). These revealed a sequence of three cultures the upper most of which could be dated in the first century A.D. with the help of the Arikamedu materials obtained from it. This also enabled the dating not only of thestratum immediately underlying it, characterised by a Megalithic burial and the typical red-and-black pottery found in association with it, but even of the lowest levels, which yielded a crude chalcolithic culture, later found to be characteristic of the Deccan and Central India.

Wheeler relinquished charge on 30 April, 1948. Before he left he had succeeded in establishing a number of firm datum lines to which the results of future excavations could be correlated. Another great achievement of his was to transform the entire character of the excavation methods followed in India by subordinating them to stratigraphical control and analyses conformably to the best international standards. The methods followed now in India are virtually those which he had introduced.

While great transformations were thus being effected in the method, outlook and scope of Indian archaeology it became involved in a number of sweeping changes which were the inevitable consequences of India's emergence as an independent State.

An immediate effect of the political revolution was to impose new boundaries on the archaeological map of India and to deprive her of almost all the sites associated with the earliest cultures in India, including not only the Harappan civilisation but the stone age industries of the Sohan valley. She equally lost the very important Gandhara sites, the homeland of one of the most interesting phases of her art history, including Charsada, Sahri-Bahlol, Takht-i-Bahi and Taxila. Organisationally, the Frontier Circle was detached from India, and the part of Panjab remaining with her was combined with Delhi to form into a separate Circle, while Orissa was added to West Bengal to form part of the reorganised Eastern Circle. The Survey itself underwent a rechristening and was given the new designation of Department of Archaeology. Another significent event which deserves mention was the enactment of the Antiquities (Export Control) Act of 1947 which prescribed penalities for exporting out of India any object more than one hundred years old without a licence from Government. Thus at last was established a legal means to ensure that the country was not denuded of her antiquarian treasures.

Other changes, even more significant, were soon to follow and as all of them were the outcome of the great political upheaval of 1947 they deserve a brief mention here. The Constitution, promulgated in 1950, made a radical change in the allocation of responsibilities between the Centre and the States. The Centre henceforth was to care only for those ancient and historical monuments and archaeological sites and remains which might be declared by Parliament to be of national importance, while to the States were allotted the responsibilities in respect of all monuments outside the category. As regards archaeological sites and remains other than monuments, the Centre and the States were vested with concurrent jurisdiction. The effect of this allocation was that the Department of archaeology was relieved of the care it had been bestowing on numerous monuments of mere local significance and became free to restrict its activities to outstanding monuments only. The centre, very rightly, was not completely absolved of its responsibilties in respect of archaeological sites, and was empowered to assert itself whenever it had reason to believe that the sites in the jurisdiction of any State were being neglected or explored in an unscientific or a harmful manner.

This redistribution of archaeological functions was followed up by the enactment in 1951 of a Central Statute declaringto be of national importance all the monuments andsites which had been protected under the Ancient Monuments Preservation Act, together with a large number of those situated in the ci-devant Indian States over which the Department of Archaeology had no jurisdiction before. An inevitable corollary of all these changes was the rapid assimilation of the archaeological work in these States into the functions of the Central Organisation. The first to be affected by the process was the former State of Baroda. Other States followed suit, and by 1953 the archaeological integration of practically the whole of India had been completed.

During this momentous period of its history the Department was fortunate in having at its head two of the ablest Directors General that were ever called upon to shed lustre on it, Dr. N.P. Chakravarti and M.S.

Vats, to whose distinguished achievements a reference has already been made. Dr. Chakravarti had taken over on 30 April 1948 and held the ferule till 30 April 1950, when it fell to Vats to assume the charge of the Department. On Vats' retirement on 2 March 1953, the office developed on its present incumbent A. Ghosh. The developments which have taken place during all these eventful years are too recent to permit an adequate treatment and are well beyond the scope of the present narrative. But it may be permissible to add that, thanks mainly to the industry, the enthusiasm, the technical competence and the knowledge which have been brought to bear, during this period, on the task of unravelling the mystery and grandeur that is India's past, the Department of Archaeology has not only been able to uphold its prestige but has proved itself to be one of the best organisations of the kind in the world. Indeed, 'today no part of the world is better served in archaeological matters than is the Republic of India'. The words are not the writer's; they come from one of the leading archaeologists of modern times.

Bust of Sir William Jones (1746-94) in Asiatic Society Kolkata

Plate II

Bust of James Prinsep (1799-1840) in Asiatic Society, Kolkata

Plate III

Meadows Taylor (1808-1876)

Plate IV

Sir Alexander Cunningham (1814-93)

Plate V

James Burgess (1832-1916)

Plate VI

Marquess Curzon of Kedleston (1859-1925)

Sir John Marshall (1876-1958)

Plate VIII

Sir Aurel Stein (1862-1943)

K. N. Dikshit (1889-1946)

Plate X

N. G. Majumdar (1893-1938)

Plate XI

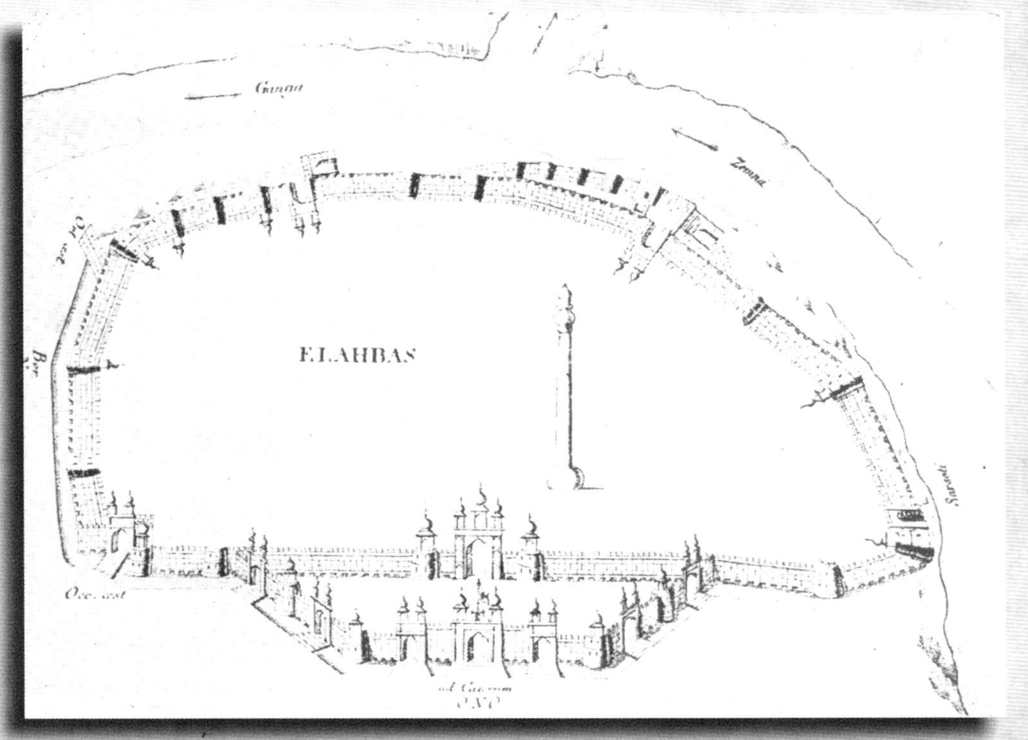

Allahabad Fort with Asokan pillar. Drawing by Joseph Tieffenthaler

Plate XII

PICTURESQUE ELEVATION of the SHIKAR-GAH, & the CELEBRATED PILLAR at DEHLI in JUNE,

Drawing by Captain Hoare of the pyramidal palace at Firuz Shah's Fort in Delhi showing the Asokan pillar

Plate XIII

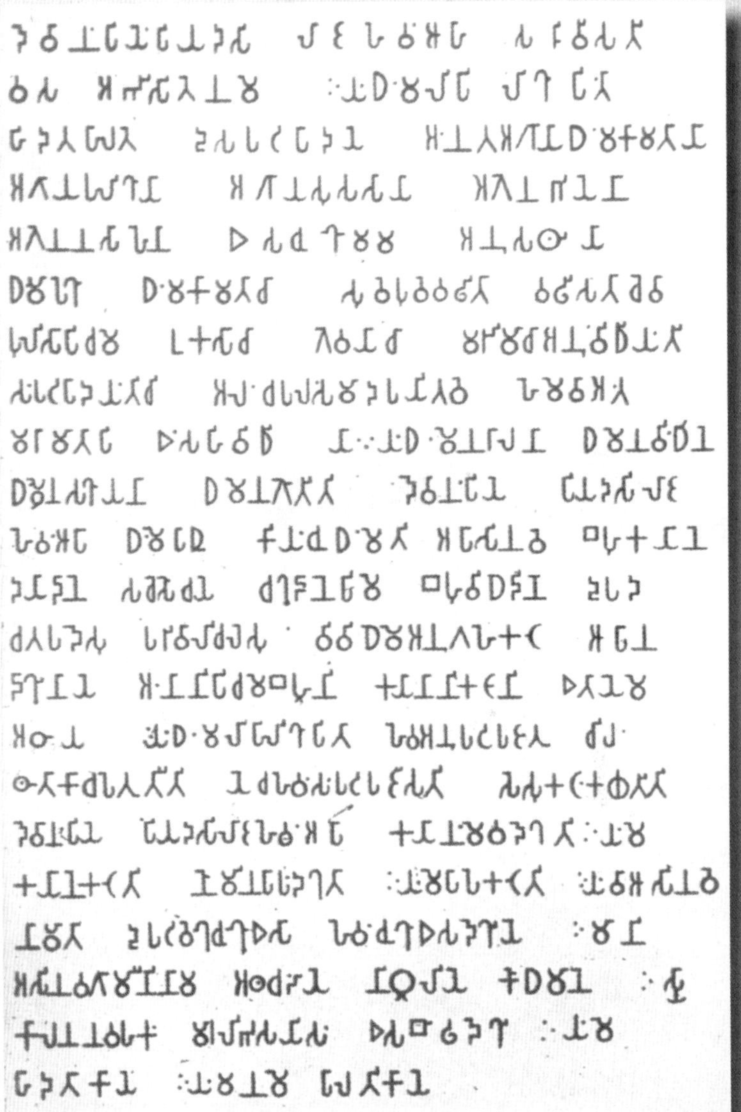

Eye-copy prepared by captain James Hoare of a portion of the Brahmi inscription on the column at Firuz Shah's Fort

Plate XIV

View of Indra-Sabha in Ellora (sketch made by Ganga Ram under the direction of Charles Warre Malet)

View of the Visvesvara temple as seen in 1825 (drawing by James Prinsep)

Plate XVI

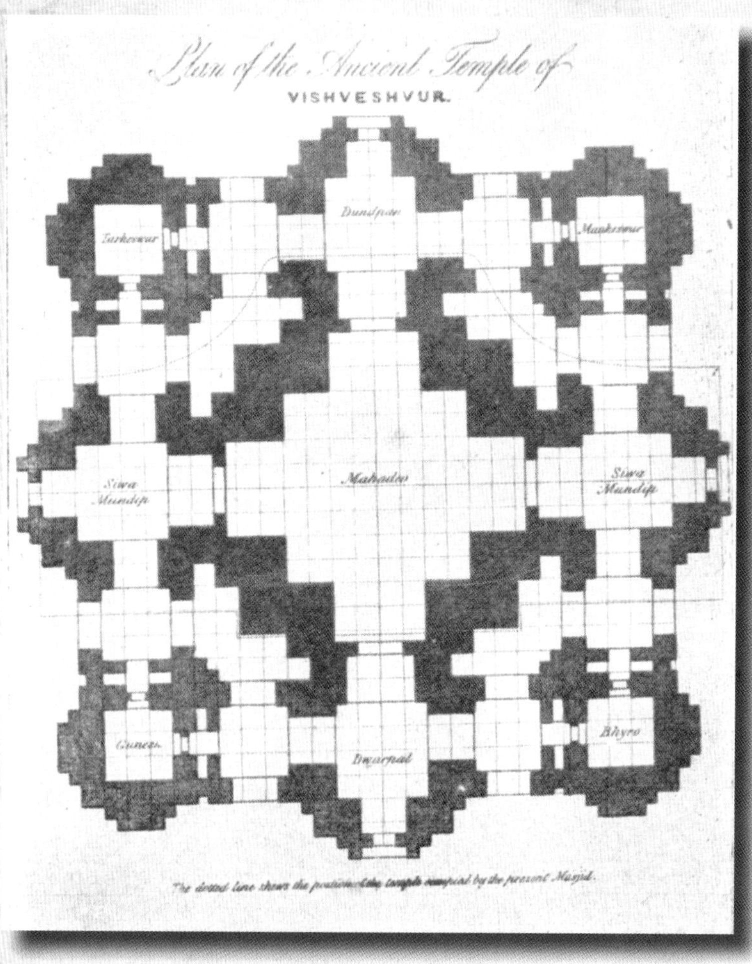

Ground-plan of the Visvesvara temple by James Prinsep

To the Right Honorable George Lord Auckland
&c &c &c

My Lord

Should your Lordship have found amusement in perusing the account in my last journal, of the discovery of Antiochus' name in an inscription sent round here last year by Mr Wathen the Chief Secretary at Bombay from Girnar a rock in the Gujerat promontory, I have now completed the deciphering of the whole inscription and have met with a passage still more extraordinary than that relating to Antiochus in which, speaking of the places where the Indian king's ordinances of religion are to be spread, occur the words

"the Greek king also by whom the Egyptian kings Ptolemaios & Antigonus and Magas :— The context is cut off: but I imagine it to be very clearly intelligible from what is preserved in the line following viz.— 'everywhere the religious ordinances of Piyadasi are made known &c —

James Prinsep's letter to Lord Auckland dated 28 March 1838, on his discovery of the names of the three Greek rulers in the Girnar Rock inscription (first page)

Plate XVIII

were a monument of
such magnitude and importance found
in Egypt we should have savans
deputed from England and France
to examine it. Here it is at our
doors and I venture to believe
Your Lordships will not permit the
opportunity to be lost of turning
it to the best account.

I have the honour to be My Lord
Your Lordships very faithful hum.

28th March 1838

J Prinsep

James Prinsep's letter to Lord Auckland (concluding portion)

Plate XIX

The Society feels that they have every reason to be highly flattered with the condescension and consideration extended to their address by the Members of Government; and although a reference to the Honorable the Court of Directors had been deemed indispensable before finally determining on the adoption of the Society's proposition for the formation of a National Museum at the cost of the State, still they entertain the most sanguine assurance of a favorable issue, under the encouragement and recommendation with which His Lordship in Council has been pleased to promise that the reference home shall be accompanied.

James Prinsep's letter to the Government dated 26 July 1837, pleading the case for a National Museum (second page)

Plate XX

Sketch of Girnar rock with Asokan inscription by Lieut. W. Postan, 1838

Plate XXI

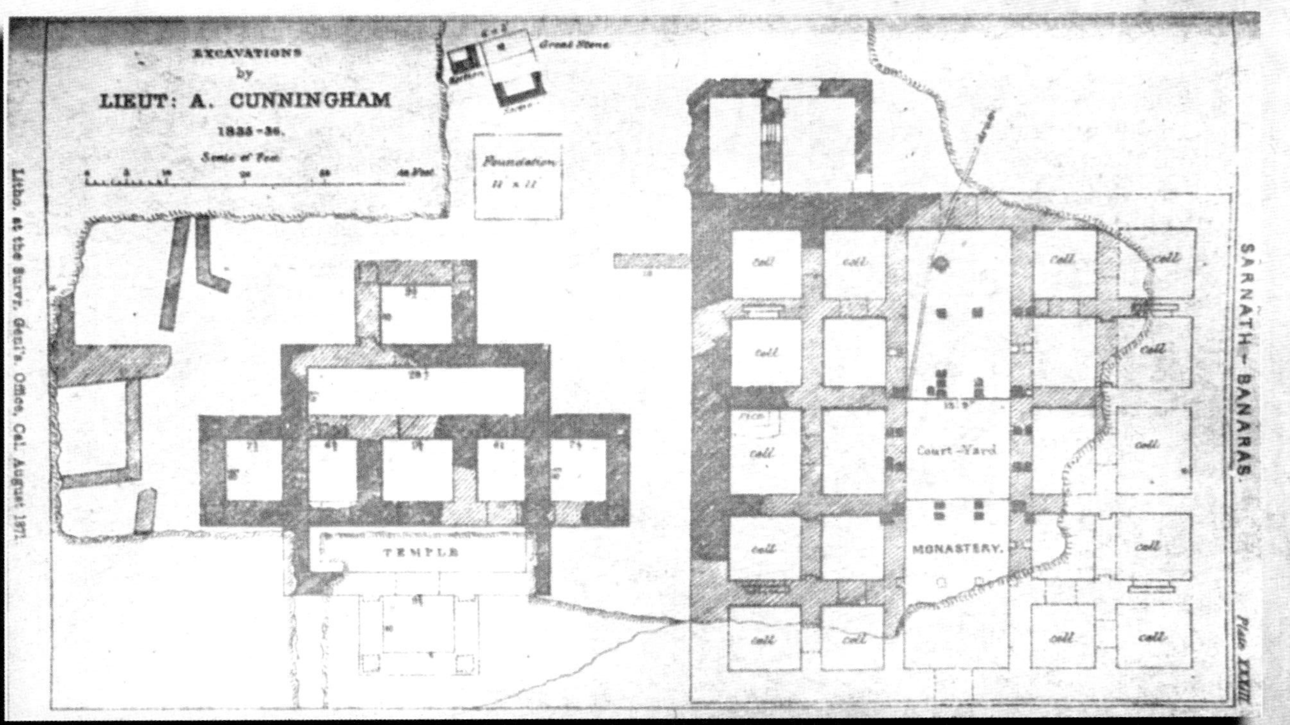

Plans illustrating Cunningham's excavations among the ruins adjoining the Dhamekh Stupa, Sarnath, 1835-36

Plate XXII

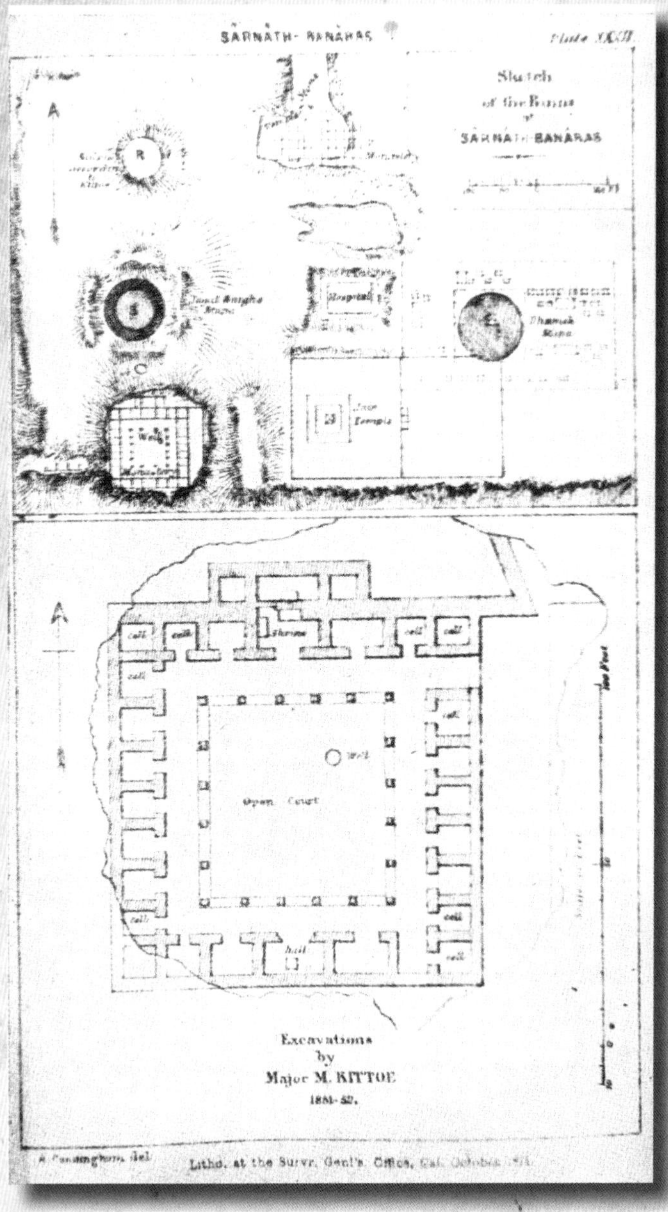

Sketch of the ruins of Sarnath by Cunningham and plan illustrating the excavations of Major Kittoe, 1851-52

Plate XXIII

East side of the Shahpoor Tumulus, showing the Granite Boundary Rocks and some of the Greenstone Boulders.

SKETCH NO. 13

South side of Shahpoor Tumulus Boundary, Granite Kolas.

Drawing of the south side of Shahpur megalith by Meadows Taylor

Plate XXIV

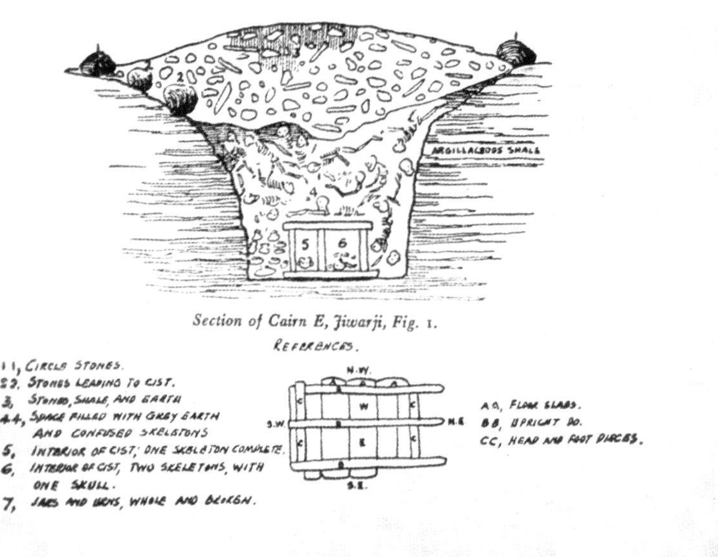

Section of Cairn E, Jiwarji, Fig. 1.

Drawing by Meadows Taylor of the Section of a Cairn

Plate XXV

Memorandum

regarding a proposed Investigation of the Archaeological remains of Upper India

---

1 – During the one hundred years of British dominion in India the Government has done little or nothing towards the preservation of its ancient monuments, which in the almost total absence of any written history form the only reliable sources of information as to the early condition of the country. Some of these monuments have already endured for ages, and are likely to last for ages still to come; but there are many others which are daily suffering from the effects of time, and which must soon disappear altogether unless preserved by the accurate drawings and faithful descriptions of the archaeologist.

2 – All that has hitherto been done towards the illustration of ancient Indian history has been due to the unaided efforts of private individuals – These researches consequently have always been desultory and unconnected and frequently incomplete, owing partly to the short stay which individual Officers usually make at any particular place, and partly to the limited leisure which could be devoted to such pursuits.

3 – Hitherto the Government has been chiefly occupied with the extension and consolidation of the Empire, but the establishment of the Trigonometrical Survey shows that it has not been unmindful of the claims of Science. It would redound equally to the honor of the British Government to institute a careful and systematic investigation of all the existing monuments of ancient India –

Memorandum by Cunningham on 'proposed archaeological investigations in India', November 1861 (extract from the first page)

Plate XXVI

7 — I believe that it would be possible to make a careful examination of all the places which I have noted during two cold seasons. The first season might be devoted to a survey of Gaya and of Rajagriha, and of all the remains in Tirhoot to the Eastward of Benares and Gorackpore; while the survey of all to the Westward of Benares would occupy the second season.

8 — I would attach to the description of each place a general survey of the site showing clearly the positions of all the existing remains with a ground plan of every building or ruin of special note, accompanied by drawings and sections of all objects of interest. It would be desirable also to have photographic views of many of the remains both of architecture and of sculpture; but to obtain these it would be necessary to have the services of a photographer. Careful facsimiles of all inscriptions would of course be made. Ancient coins would also be collected on each site; and all the local traditions would be noted down and compared. The description of each place, with all its accompanying drawings and illustrations would be complete in itself; and the whole when finished would form a detailed and accurate account of the archaeological remains of Upper India.

A. Cunningham, Colonel
Engineers.

Cunningham's memorandum on archaeological investigations (concluding paragraphs)

Plate XXVII

It is true that in 1844, on a representation from the Royal Asiatic Society, and in 1847, in accordance with detailed suggestions from Lord Hardinge, the Court of Directors gave a liberal sanction to certain arrangements for examining, delineating, & recording some of the chief antiquities of India. But for one reason or another, – mainly perhaps owing to the Officer entrusted ~~appointed~~ with ~~to~~ the task having other work to do, & owing to his early death, very little seems to have resulted from this endeavor. A few drawings and some remains of antiquities, ~~in Western India~~ were transmitted to the India House, and some fifteen or twenty papers were contributed by Major Kittoe and Major Cunningham to the Journals of the Asiatic Society:

Canning's Minute on the setting up of an Archaeological Survey, 20 January 1862 (extract showing additions made in his own hand)

It would be premature to determine how the results of Colonel Cunningham's labors should be dealt with; but whilst the Government would of course retain a proprietary right in them for its own purposes I recommend that the interests of Colonel Cunningham should be considered in the terms upon which they may be furnished to the Public.

Canning

January 22d. 1862.

Canning's Minute (concluding portion)

No. 24
Fort William
Public Works Deptt
General
Establt
The 31st January 1862
D/ Appointment

Colonel A Cunningham of Engineers is appointed Archaeological Surveyor to the Govt of India, for employment in Behar and elsewhere, with effect from 1st Decr last

Draft gazette notification announcing Cunningham's appointment as Archaeological Surveyor

Plate XXX

Sketch map of Northern India by Cunningham showing important historical sites

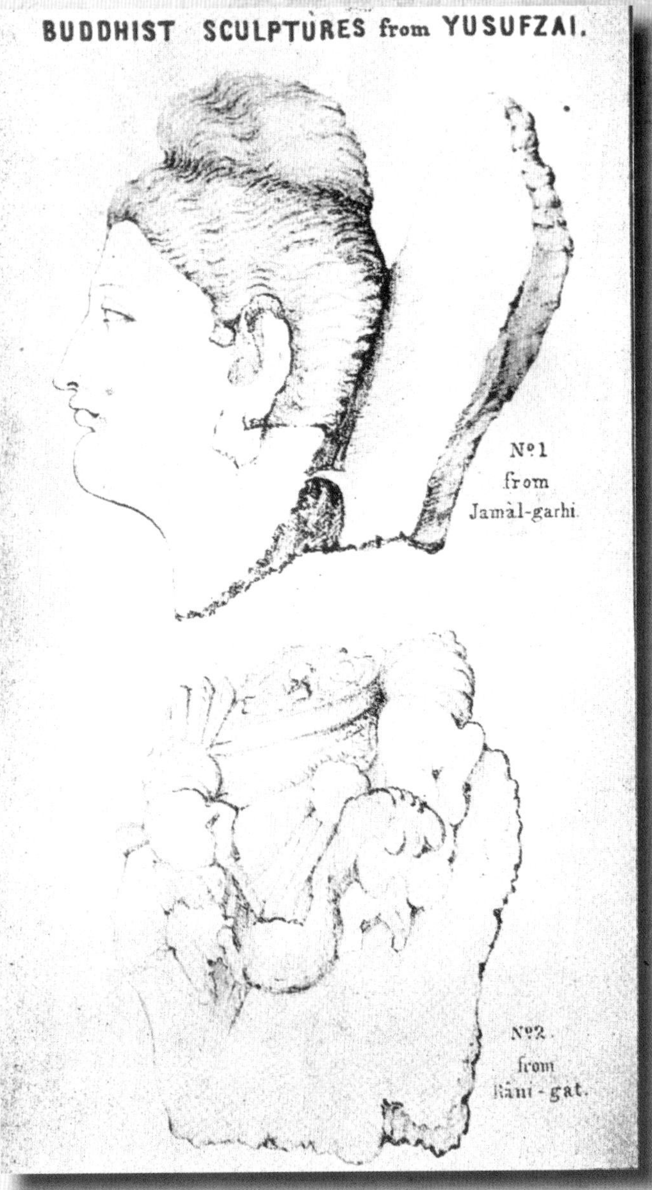

Finds from Yasufzai, season 1863-64, drawing by Cunningham

Plate XXXII

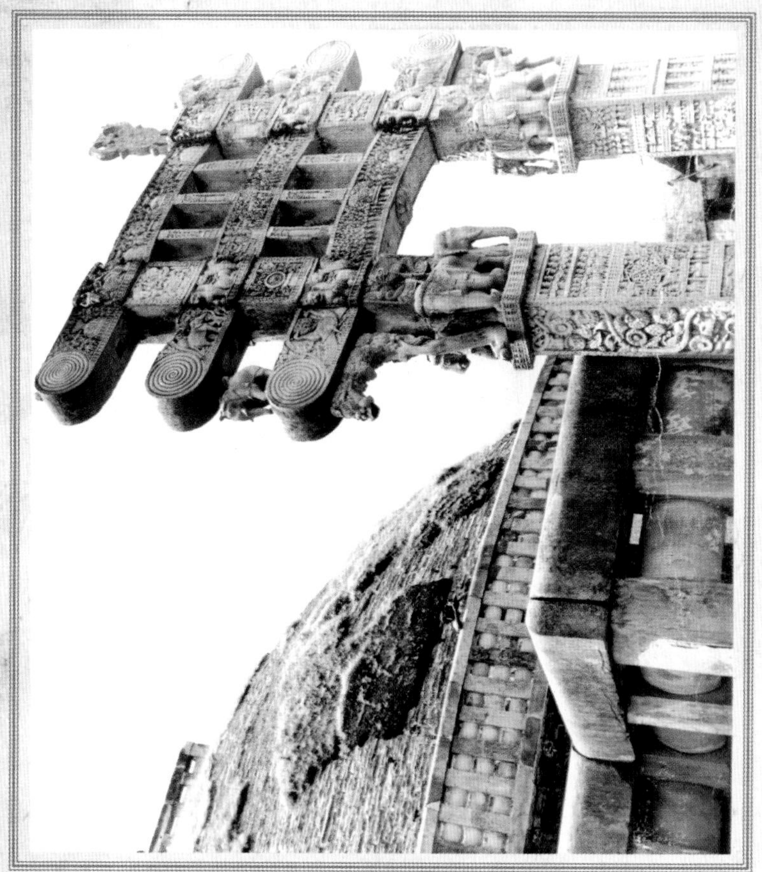

Eastern gateway of Sanchi Stupa (from a drawing reproduced in the Illustrated London News, 5 March 1870)

Plate XXXIII

Temple of Martanda, Kashmir (from a drawing reproduced in the Illustrated London News, 5 March 1870)

Plate XXXIV

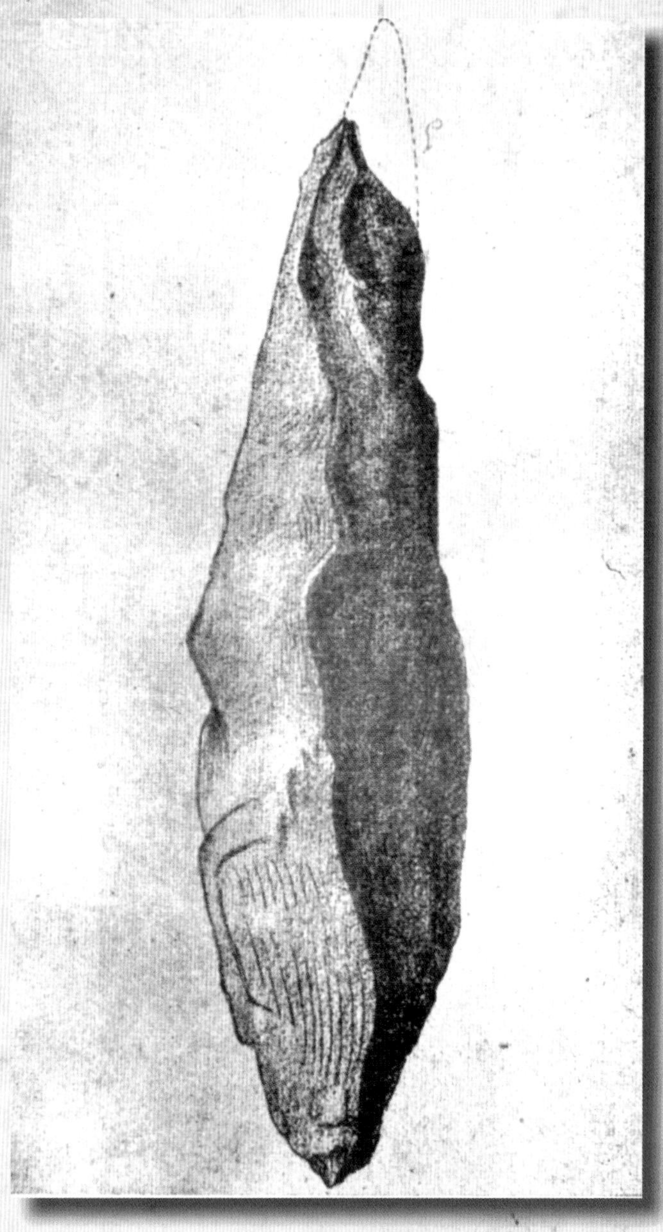

The first palaeolith found by Robert Bruce Foote at Pallavaram

But, be that as it may I think the time is come when a great & enlightened Govt. can no longer neglect contributing to the Archaeological literature of the World – the result of systematic investigation into Monuments and Remains, which perhaps are not equalled ~~in any part of the world~~ for their historical and archaeological value.

An extract from Lord Mayo's Minute dated 30 May 1870

Should this project
be entertained by my Colleagues
I would recommend that Gen.
Cunningham should be, at
once communicated with on
the subject and perhaps
it would be better to as-
certain his opinion before
the various Asiatic &
Oriental Societies both
in India & Europe were
invited to give their opinion

Mayo

Mayo's Minute of 30 May 1870 (concluding portion)

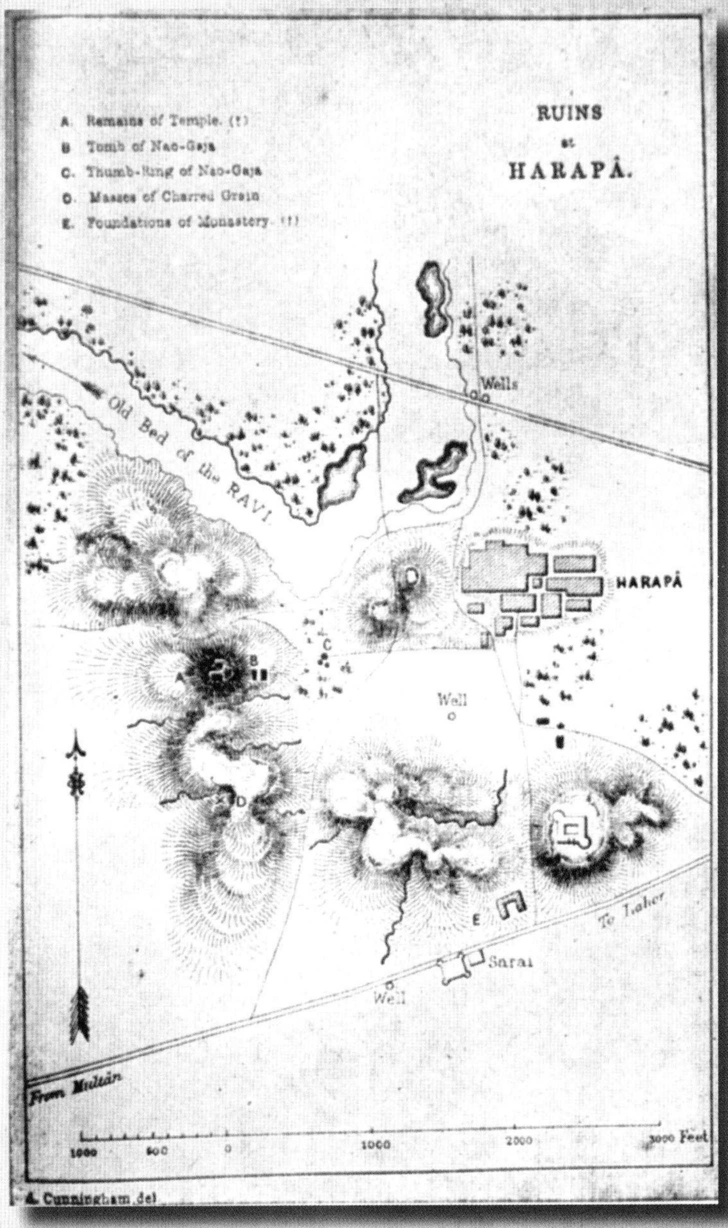

Plan by Cunningham of the ruins at Harappa (season 1872-1873)

Plate XXXVIII

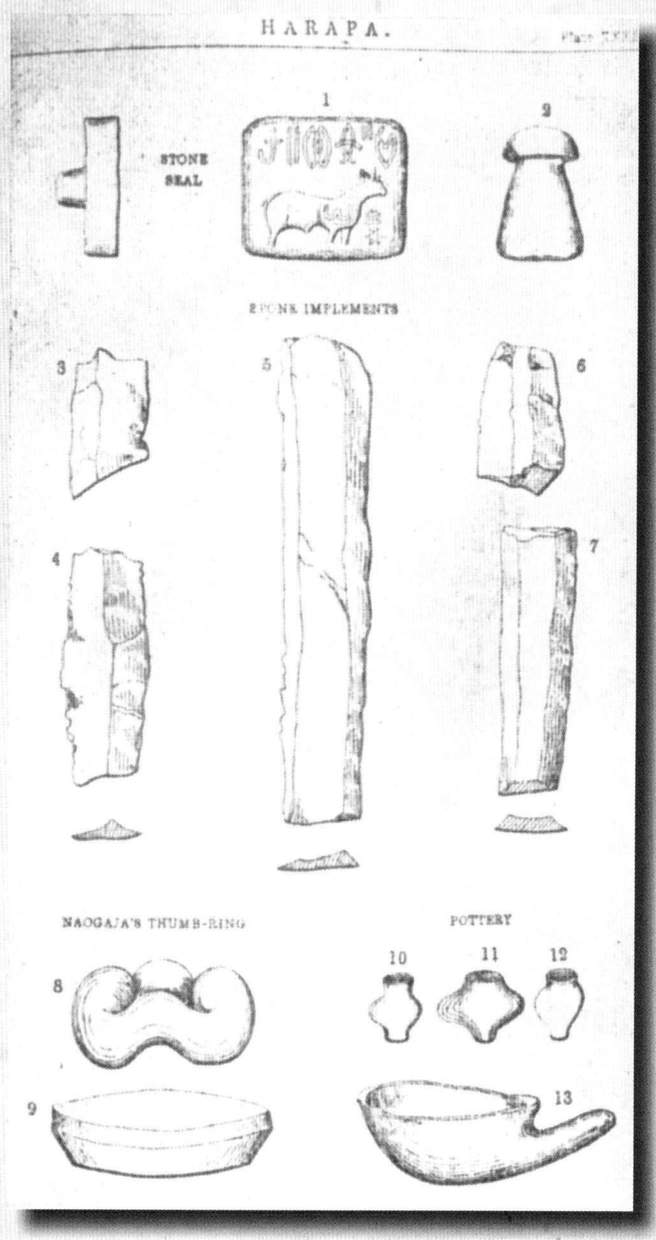

Finds from Harappa, season 1872-1873 (drawing by Cunningham)

Bhita: Terracotta disk, believed to be a scene from Kalidasa's Sakuntala

Plate XL

Jaulian: Buddha image

Taxila: Air view of Sirkap, showing town-planning conforming to the Hippodamian model

Plate XLII

Mohenjo-Daro: General view of streets and houses

Plate XLIII

Harappa: Parallel walls, granary area

Plate XLIV

Paharpur: main temple (general view)

Plate XLV

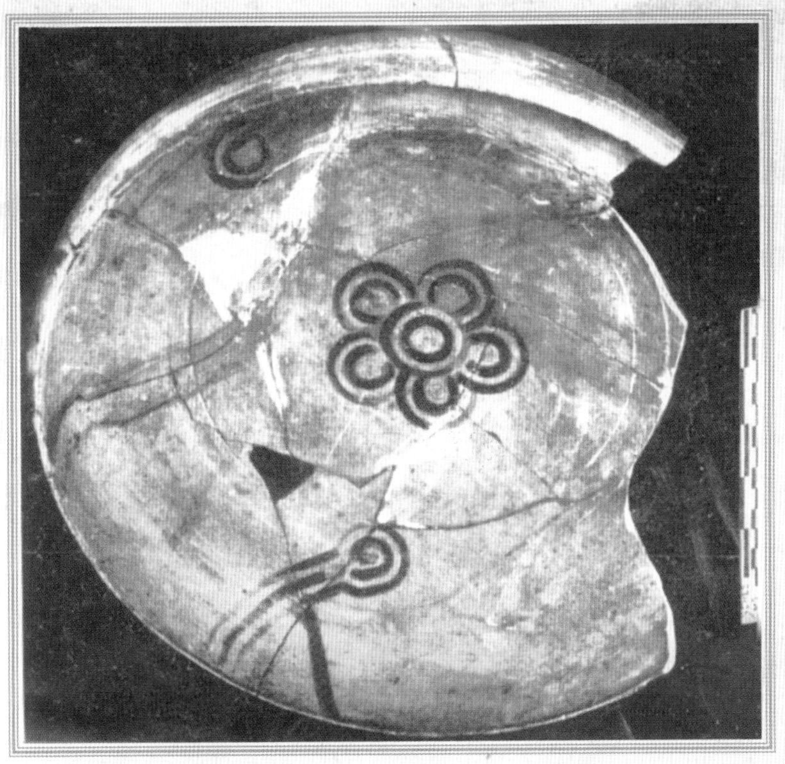

Ahichchhatra: Painted Grey ware

Plate XLVI

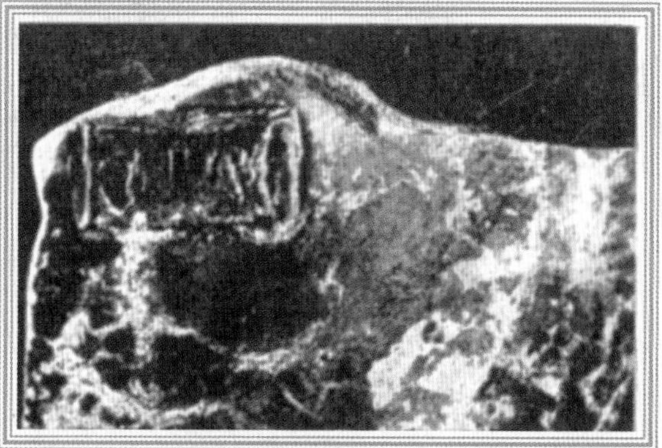

Arikamedu: Specimens of Arretine ware

Harappa: Skeleton in cemetery R 37 illustrating extended burial

Plate XLVIII

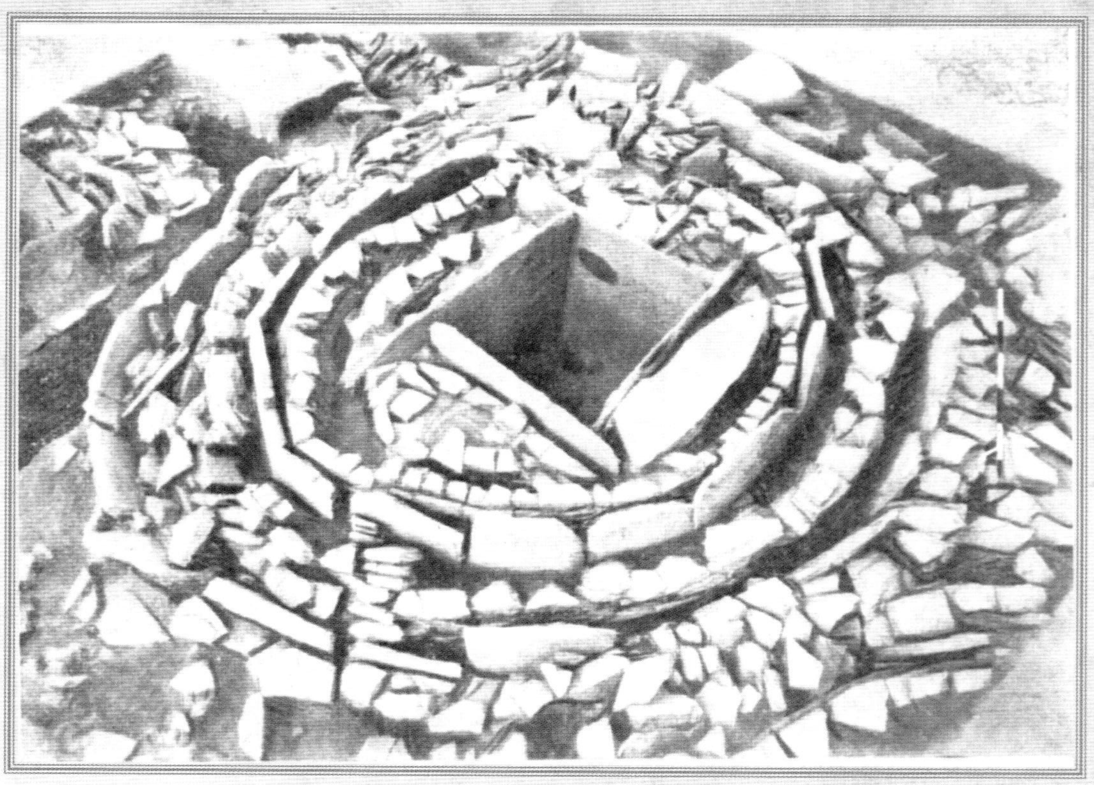

Brahmagiri: Megalithic cist

SOURINDRANATH ROY

ARCHIVIST AND HISTORIAN

Sourindranath Roy

SOURINDRANATH ROY

ARCHIVIST AND HISTORIAN

George M Moraes

THE LATE MR. SOURINDRANATH ROY - "Sourin" as he was affectionately known among his friends - had undertaken to share with me the editorial responsibility for the present journal. He suggested its name *India Past and Present* and volunteered to conduct a column on diverse historical topics under the caption: *Notes and Queries*. "It may be run", he wrote in his letter dated Christmas 1982 eleven days before he passed away on January 5, "as a forum for those being exercised by genuine curiosity about historical matters as also for those who are in a position to answer them. It will, if started, I venture to believe, remove a long-felt want:" He also gave me the names of the scholars who could be depended upon to support the journal with their contributions but advised that it should not come out unless it was ahead of articles for at least two issues.

A professional archivist who could say the last word on his subject, he was also *sans pareil* in matters historical to which he happened to apply his genius, being capable of forestalling scholars in their own exclusive and chosen fields of study. Though Marxist in his leanings, he would not take Marx on trust. In his remarkable article "Recent Trends in Indian Research Activities in Modern Indian History," in which he estimates at their true worth works produced of late under Marxist inspiration, he declared that in such works of familiar Marxist interpretation theoretical speculation overrode objective analysis of evidence. A classical scholar combining knowledge of Greek, Latin and Sanskrit, he must have appreciated the declaration of Thucydides that as regards material facts, when he had not been an eyewitness himself, he had investigated with the utmost accuracy attainable every detail he had taken at second hand. Roy must have clasped to his heart the principles of genuine history set down by Cicero: "that it is the first law of history that it dare say nothing which is false nor fear to utter anything that is true, in order that there may be no suspicion either of partiality or hostility in the writer." He must have been highly impressed by the twin counsel of our own classical historian Kalhana who wished that history should be, interestingly written and truthfully told.

A man of principles, Roy stayed on an even keel, not taken off his feet by a blind admiration for anything. An agnostic, he yet held that if God's existence cannot be proved, neither can God's non-existence. Inclined towards Communism, he yet contended that if a confessional State cannot be secular, nor can any of the States that have come under the heel of Communism. "For, in the place of the old God of the popular creeds, Communism has placed on the altar an entirely new deity bearing the high-sounding name of Dialectical Materialism, a deity, more aggressive, more ruthless and far more intolerant" that anything that has so far struck the human mind. ("Atheism as a Way of Life", *The Radical Humanist*, June 1981, pp. 27-29 under the pen-name of Ulysses Young).

A tribute paid to Roy by Professor Sudhir Ranjan Das in his letter to me of 6 July merits permanent record, bringing out as it does his dominant characteristic:

> I have been very much moved by your letter bearing a touching reference to Sourinda who was to me a most revered academic personality, possessing a profound and penetrating power of

seeing into and understanding diverse and perplexing trends in the history of our country. I have hardly come across a person of his stature in our academic circles. As you know, his intensive research encompassed the whole range of Indian history with all nicety and perfection. His was an analytical mind hardly enduring, let alone compromising with, any trash historical writings, about which you have made a pointed reference in your letter… His demise has been an irreparable loss to us all.

Lord Acton said that impartial history can have no friends. Roy must have offended quite a few. Non-partisan historians can seldom be popular.

Archivist

Born on 16 June 1911 at Lohagara, Jessore District, now in Bangladesh, Roy was a brilliant product of the Presidency College, Calcutta, and the Calcutta University. He scored both his B.A. and M.A. with distinction. Yet he had a chequered career. He started from the lowest echelon, that of an Assistant, when he joined in 1939 the Imperial Records Department, now the National Archives of India. It was only by slow degrees that he rose to become the Deputy Director of Archives when in an officiating capacity he had occasion to occupy the highest post-that of Director of Archives-from September 1960 to December 1961.

At his entry into the Archives he was confronted by an uncharted sea of documents. Archives-keeping at his time had sunk to its lowest depth, signifying, in his own words, "no more than mere keeping of inactive documents." A colossal task awaited him. He rose equal to it. He immediately started surveying the records, a practice, diligently pursued over the years, made him a legend. When

Surendranath Sen joined in as Director soon after and embarked on a vast programme of indexing, calendaring and publishing of documents with a view to making the archives serviceable, Roy became his trusted and indispensable aide. Under this programme two volumes were published of detailed indexes to the Land Revenue Records, 1830-1859 and materials were prepared for a third volume relating to the proceedings of the Select Committee and the Secret Department 1756-1780, dealing with country as well as foreign powers.

The calendaring was speeded up of what is called Persian Correspondence, an important series consisting of correspondence maintained in Persian between the Company's servants and the Indian Princes and notables as also foreign powers. He was entirely responsible for the preparation of biographical and historical notes to the texts of documents published. He was also the brain behind the project of publishing selected documents from the National Archives written in the principal Indian Languages. It fell to his lot to trace the Sanskrit documents for this series to decipher and transcribe the text, to provide a full critical apparatus for each document to prepare its English translation, to compile detailed notes on obscure names, words and expressions occurring therein, and to select material for the introduction of the volume for being written by the Director.

This volume, consisting of twenty-five documents, was published by G.N. Jha Institute, Allahabad in 1951 under the title *Sanskrit Documents 1778-1857*. It begins with two memoranda sent to the British Government through Thompson, Warren Hastings' attorney in India. Thompson approached the Governor-General-in-Council and the latter agreed to act as post office. The memoranda refer to the specific acts of Hastings which were particularly calculated to benefit the pilgrims to Banaras, e.g. the abolition of undue and illegal exactions of the Gangaputras or officiating priests, facilities for free and unrestricted performance of religious rites, the appointment of the upright Ali Ibrahim Khan as Chief Magistrate of Banaras, and the construction of a *naubatkhana* or musical gallery near the gateway of the Visvanatha Temple, an act of homage which was very much appreciated, coming as it did from a Christian ruler. The Pandits were grateful to Hastings for his patronage of Sanskrit learning and speak of the rare kindness they received at his hands during his second visit to the holy city.

The fourth document is a letter (dated 2 March 1971) from Bahuji Maharaj, head of the Maharaj sect at Surat, styling herself Gosvamini Maharajni, who is soliciting the indulgence of Lord Cornwallis, the Governor General, to open correspondence with him. She makes the important observation that, owing to the persecution of the sect in the place of its origin, Muttra, its headquarters had to be shifted to Surat. She praises the English, "through (whose) power and rule religious prejudice disappeared.

"Document IX is a letter in which the grateful priests, abbots, recluses, Vaishnavas, Brahmanas, and the royal preceptor of Puri, headed by Krishna Chandra Mahapatra, pay a humble tribute to Lord Wellesley for his peaceful annexation of Orissa. They assure him of their prayers "night and day to God that the supremacy of the English power may last for ever...." During the second Maratha War, it was the deliberate policy of Wellesley to cultivate the people of Cuttack to wrest this Maratha province. He even engaged the services of a famous Bengali pandit to reassure the people that "the British Government not only permits the Hindus to enjoy the free exercise of their religion, but manifests the greatest degree of benevolence, favour and indulgence towards them." And to show that the hope they had expressed in their letter that before long pilgrims from all over would pour into the holy city may not be in vain, the English abolished the tax of eleven rupees which the Maratha Government used to levy on each pilgrim. As a result, there was such an influx of pilgrims that it was found necessary to prohibit export of foodgrains from the province.

There are diplomatic and legal documents included in the volume as also petitions and memorials. The notes appended to the documents by Roy are an eloquent testimony to his wide-ranging scholarship, adding as they do so much to our knowledge. They are a model worthy to be followed by any editor. Professor V. Raghavan was not exaggerating a bit when he remarked in his review of the book (*The Hindu* June 22, 1952) that the documents could not have been better edited.

Lastly, Roy had a major share in editing *The Browne Correspondence 1782-85* (National Archives of India, 1960, 363 pp.) inasmuch as it was he who discovered the volume containing the correspondence, located the material missing from the volume, provided the text with full critical notes, compiled detailed notes on personal and place names, technical terms and historical allusions occurring in the text, and collected the material from a wide variety of sources for the introduction to the volume.

Major James Browne was chosen by Warren Hastings for the onerous task of restoring Shah Alam's authority during the struggle for the control of Delhi and the Emperor among the chief claimants for power: Mirza Shafi Khan, Afrasiab Khan, Najab Quli Khan and Muhammad Beg Hamdani. Browne, however, proved a poor judge of character. When in February 1784 he met Shah Alam and Afrasiab

Khan, who had succeeded to the ministership, and was shown Sindia's letters proposing an alliance against the English, he wrote to Hastings that letters "were of a quality to convey light to the blind and hearing to the deaf." Hastings who confident of Sindia's loyalty dismissed the letters as no more than forgeries. Even if Sindia sought to secure control of affairs in Delhi, it did not necessarily mean hostility towards the English. Eventually, Shah Alam was brought under his control and Sir John Macpherson, the successor of Hastings, seeing the futility of maintaining two envoys, one at Gwalior and the other at Delhi, recalled Browne on 1 March 1783. When the latter delayed his departure, he sent him a peremptory order to return, and Browne had his audience of dismissal with the *roifaineant* on April 1785.

Division of Archives

A little before Partition in 1947, the records of the Central Government were in imminent danger of physical division between the incipient States of Pakistan and India. It was contended on behalf of the former that "all records of Muslim interest prior to the year 1857 should be given to the Pakistan Government and all those subsequent to that year may be kept by the Hindustan Government." It would be open to either of the emerging states to arrange copies to be taken of the documents in their possession. And in this way it would be possible to maintain in both the countries the continuity of the original series as before. But the physical division should take place immediately. Pakistan sought to support its viewpoint, asserting that "instances of countries could be cited where the division of records did take place on partitioning of the country,"

In the reply which he prepared, Roy called off the Pakistani bluff by stating that there is not a single instance of a country where physical division of the archives has taken place consequent on partition. The reason is that any attempt at dividing the Central records would make both the emerging collections lose their archival and evidential value. An archival collection is an inter-related series, and accordingly the importance of keeping an archival series intact has long been recognized in European countries. Nearer home, the Government of India did not surrender the archives to the Malay States when it ceased to administer these States. Neither did it hand over to the Dutch the records relating to Java when this island was restored to the latter. Nor were the Central records relating to Burma transferred from Delhi to Rangoon on Burma's separation from India.

The Imperial Records Department, the Central Archives, was thus saved thanks to the presence on the spot of a competent officer who had made, as he himself says, "a special study of international practices with regard to the treatment of archives affected by political changes and territorial redistribution." The memorandum of Roy on the basis of which the division of the archives of the undivided Government of India was forestalled is far more conclusive—and the best attempt so far—than the near classic study: "Effect of Changes of Sovereignty on Archives" in the *American Archives*, July 1942. As the same Journal aptly remarked in its issue of October 1947, "the division of files and records between India and Pakistan (was) one of the biggest problems confronting the Partition Council." It is thus all the more creditable that Roy should have solved the problem in the midst of the prevailing gloom yielding to despair that there was no way of saving the Central Archives from being partitioned when the country itself was doomed to share this fate.

Archival Legislation

Roy was again able to give of his best when in his capacity as officiating Director of Archives (1960-61) he became *ipso facto*

Secretary of the Committee appointed in August 1959 to advise the Government regarding the desirability or otherwise of making a law applicable to archives in India, and produced a masterly report on archival legislation. (Committee on Archival Legislation, 1959, *Report*, New Delhi, National Archives of India, 1960, 143 + ivpp.). In his view the National Archives of India should have under its control the repositories not only of the ministries but also of such record-creating bodies as (1) Departments subordinate to the Secretariat or the Attached Offices (namely, those having all-India jurisdiction, those whose jurisdiction affects an entire State or a bigger region embracing several States, those whose activities are limited to a small area like a division or district, small units or field offices serving a very small area like a sub-division, town or even a village, and educational or research institutions run by a Government Department); (2) Bodies outside the Secretariat, but forming an integral part of the Central Government set-up (e.g., the Union Public Service Commission, the Comptroller and Auditor-General, the Planning Commission, the Prime Minister's Secretariat, the President's Secretariat and the Cabinet Secretariat); (3) Boards, Committees, Commissions etc., set up under the authority of the Government of India; (4) Statutory bodies of All-India character; (5) National Enterprises and Undertakings; (6) Parliament (including Lok Sabha and Rajya Sabha Secretariats as well as the Secretariats of all legislative bodies of pre-Independent days as also those emanating from the Constituent Assembly); (7) The Supreme Court except that the Court would enjoy the freedom in full measure to deal with its own records subject, however, to a statutory obligation to select and preserve records of permanent value in accordance with accepted standards.

It was only natural that a fundamental principle of archives keeping be enforced in all public officers, making it obligatory to keep their records arranged in the original order of their creation, to refrain from disturbing that order on any account and from dividing the records for reasons of any organizational or jurisdictional change. The filing practice should also follow a set pattern, ensuring that a file's contents are adequately described by its title, no file is used to house papers on a subject other than it was originally intended to deal with, that files dealing with policy decisions are not cluttered with papers relating to particular applications of those decisions, and that on no account matters of mere routine are allowed entry into a regular file of any category whatever.

The records in public offices should be subjected to a first review not later than five years after they have passed out of active use and be destroyed if found useless for their own departmental purposes. The criterion to be used while reviewing a file is whether the file is likely to be needed should a circumstance similar to that which led to its origin happen to arise again. The documents surviving the first review should be subjected to a second review when they reach the 25th year and any paper deemed unworthy of further retention at this stage should be disposed of. Care, however, should be taken to see that the files containing papers which are important, even if indirectly, as sources of any aspect of history (political, military, social, economic, etc.) or which are or may prove to be of biographical interest are not destroyed. The files surviving the second review should be regarded as mature for retirement and should be transferred immediately to the National Archives of India. It is the duty of the National Archives to assist the Departments in selecting the records and ensure their permanent preservation under its custody.

The States should also enact laws providing for all public bodies under their control and this legislation should cover State legislatures, High Courts and other Courts and the local governments

(District Boards, Municipalities etc.), provision being made in each case for their management, appraisal, retirement and accessibility.

As to private archives it is best that their preservation and management are left to private initiative which may where necessary be reinforced by state-aid, flowing either from the Centre or from the States in which they are situated. Universities, learned societies, libraries and historical societies should also be encouraged to acquire and arrange for the preservation of collections, worthy of permanent preservation. Financial assistance may be granted to them as and when called for.

It should be said in appreciation of the report that its eagle eye has left no record-creating agency, public or private, out of its ken. The legislation intended to be framed on the basis of this report would have saved the immense archival wealth of the nation which in the absence of proper safeguards is left to perish every moment.

Archival Estrays

In his talk entitled "Unimportant Documents" in the series "The National Archives of India", broadcast from the Delhi Station of the All India Radio 1959 (*An introduction to National Archives*, pp. 20-26) Roy stresses the importance of private archives and collections in elucidating the history of a people during the period to which they relate. A letter written on the spur of the moment has less chance of being a deliberate lie than a dressed up document meant for official use or popular consumption. And more often than not the veil that separates us from character and personality, in the past can be lifted only by means of such informal writing and history made more readable and meaningful. Not that every piece of writing should be preserved, but while throwing away a paper let the archivist's warning be remembered that "a document frequently serves purposes beyond the dream of its owner, that a scrap of paper which makes no sense taken singly may reveal a sensational story when read in its proper context, that even a trifle may turn out to be tremendous."

Efforts have been made since Independence and are still continuing to retrieve our archival treasures that found their way in the past to foreign countries. In his paper, "The Problem of Archival Estrays," (*IA*, VII (1953), pp. 14-28, 151-61) Roy brings his incisive mind to bear on the loss of value the documents have suffered in lying detached from their original sources. The reason for this is the organic character of an archival collection. In an archive the documents stand to each other in the same relation as the events of which they are the reflex. They follow the order of these events and become related to each other by the same syllogistic necessity that brought together the events themselves. And it is from the relation in which the documents stand in a series that it is possible to write history, the documents haphazardly arranged being useless for the purpose. Ernst Posner has truly remarked, "While a picture that is taken from the walls of a museum has never been an integral part of a collection to which it belonged and will have the same value whether it hangs in Vienna or in Prague, records that are torn from the body of which they are an organic part lose in value and meaning."

Posner thought highly of Roy's contribution to the subject of archival estrays and wrote that the articles "constitute the soundest kind of thinking on the problem and add significantly to the body of archival theory." High praise indeed.

A large part of the material, however, especially relating to Ancient India, consists of documents which are no more than estrays from what were once genuine archival collections. But they possess no discernible links with the collection to which they originally belonged. Can history be deduced from such documents?

In his preface to Dr. Bahadur Chand Chhabra's *Diplomatic of Sanskrit Copper-plates* (New Delhi, National Archives of India, 1961, 23pp + 7 pls.) where Roy discusses this question, he avows that what the historian can make do under the circumstances is to see if he can establish the authenticity of these records. This he can accomplish by calling to his aid the sciences of Diplomatic and Epigraphy. The former compares one document with another with regard to their form, style and characteristic conventional phraseology with a view to dividing the sheep from the goats. The latter deals with the interpretation of the contents of a record, taking into consideration its language, palaeography and orthography. As Roy observes explaining the principle on which the science of diplomatic works:

> It is general experience that documents having a common source, place and date of origin tend to conform almost to identical pattern, a pattern which reveals itself not only in the structure of their text and the sequence of the different parts of which it is composed, but in the very phraseology and the formulary used, in the methods of engrossing, validation, dating and conveyancing in the style of writing, in the manner of arranging the text on the sheets on which it is written and even in the way in which the sheets are folded. It is the business of Diplomatic to study to patterns reflected in various type of documents and to determine the formal characteristics of each type. These characteristics, when precisely determinated, make possible careful comparison of documents of unknown

authorship, provenance or date with those whose authenticity is beyond doubt, and are thus of utmost help in identifying the former.

Roy though that, if administrative history was not making any progress, it was due to our long neglect of the science of documentary criticism. Criticism of documents inevitably leads the student to the study of the organisation that produced them.

Path-Finders

Roy's last contribution to archival science was his well-written "Four Path-finders : A Tribute to Flower, Jenkinson, Buck and Sen." (*IA*, Vol. XIV (1961-62), pp.1-21). All the four had struggled to make the study of archives a scientific discipline and to win for the record-keeper's craft the dignity of a profession.

This was the time when under the leadership of Tout, Pollard, Poole and Maitland, history teaching in British universities was being brought into closer relationship with research among primary sources. The result was that students in large numbers started flocking to the archives, perceiving the advantage of consulting records lying in proper sequence and order as is found only in these repositories. This was in contrast to the practice of consulting only printed selections which not unoften ran the risk of having been torn out of their context. The archives themselves benefited from the new vogue. Greater emphasis began to be placed on conserving the archives in their original and natural order than breaking them up or "methodising" to suit the changing mood of the moment. At the same time it came to be realized that the first duty of the archivist was to make his materials readily available to their users, leading to a radical expansion of the publication programme of the Record Office. Of this new orientation the leading lights in the West were Cyril Thomas Flower, Hilary Jenkinson and Solon Justus Buck.

Of a legal turn of mind, Cyril Thomas Flower (1879-1961), a medievalist of repute, was attracted by the Curia Regis Rolls of which he copied and edited thirteen volumes with meticulous care. Equally celebrated are his *Public Works in Medieval Law*. These editorial enterprises provided the necessary background for the long-range and comprehensive studies of Medieval England which were published later by other scholars.

Charles Hilary Jenkinson (1882-1961) was from his early days interested in tracing the vagaries of the documentary hand and the changing forms of the public record, a curiosity which, when developed, led to the formulation of the cognate science of diplomatic and palaeography. The science of sigillography also owes its development in England to his scholarly interest in the problems of repairing and conserving seals in decay. He discovered the basic principles of archives-keeping while engaged in listing and arranging the Exchequer of Receipts records, a task which started him on the investigation of the original arrangement of the Rolls. These basic principles became the corner-stone of his classic Manual of Archive Administration (1922) which has since been accepted as the most authoritative guide for archive-work in the English-speaking world. He played an important part along with collaborators such as Flower in the foundation of the British Records Association (1932) for educating public opinion in the conservation of historical records. Thanks to its efforts local repositories have been opened throughout England, drawing into their custody every variety of local records.

Solon Justus Buck (1884-1962) solved the problem of arranging the huge mass of records of the Federal Government of U.S.A. housed in the National Archives in a consultable manner, providing them with keys and guides. Under the 'Record Group' concept a unified body of records is set up in accordance with the principle of provenance and this body is usually conterminous with the total archival assets of a record-creating agency. Every document in the National Archives is physically integrated with one or other of the groups. Each group is provided with a 'registration sheet' indicating its provenance, its history, its chronological range and the scope and nature of its contents. And the reference to the records is facilitated by the check-listing and the compilation of the inventories, replacing the old and slow process of calendaring and descriptive listing of the documents.

An equal of his Western contemporaries, Surendranath Sen (1890-1962) raised the Central Archives, now the National Archives of India, from a mere store of inactive documents to the position it enjoys today as a centre of historical research. Sen was opposed to any theoretical approach to history, maintaining that no formula of the present could be of use in recapturing the past. And emphasizing the value of original sources, he got the policy of the Government changed by throwing open the Central Archives to all genuine seekers of knowledge. This was a measure which had the same effect as the opening of the Vatican Archives (1881) and the Public Record Office, London (1886), had on historical studies in Europe.

As already demonstrated, Sen owed his success largely to Roy's genius, a fact which ranks the latter among the four path-finders, being the fifth, though in a spirit of self-abnegation, so characteristic of him, he let his chief have the entire credit.

Historian

Roy commenced research in Indian history early in life when he undertook to examine under the guidance of Professor H.C. Raychaudhuri of the Calcutta University the attempt of Bhattasali to bring forward the date of the accession of Chandragupta Maurya to 313 B.C. from *c* 324-23 B.C.— the accepted date. The results of this investigation were published in an article contributed to *Indian Historical Quarterly*, Vol. XI (1934), pp. 211-22, under the caption "Date of the First Maurya Emperor".

Bhattasali had argued that Aśoka's accession took place 214 years after the Nirvāṇa of the Buddha which occurred in 477 B.C. Aśoka must therefore have come to the throne in 264/263 B.C. Adding to 264/263 B.C. forty-nine years filled by the reigns of Chandragupta and Bindusāra, twenty-four and twenty-five to be exact, we get 313 B.C. as the first regnal year of Chandragupta. The argument, however, is fallacious as Bhattasali uses simultaneously two systems of chronology.

According to the *Mahāvaṁśa* Bindusāra ruled for twenty-eight years, while the Purāṇas give him a rule of twenty-five years only. We cannot accept and reject the validity of the *Mahāvaṁśa* tradition, as Bhattasali is doing, in accepting 264 years and rejecting 28. If we reject the one, Roy rightly contends, we should reject the other also. Moreover, it is still to be proved that the Nirvāṇa took place in 477 B.C. Hardly any evidence can be adduced in favour of any possible existence of such a reckoning.

The second argument for advancing the accession of Chandragupta is that Aśoka's Rock Edict XIII should be dated 248/247 B.C. having been promulgated not earlier than the twelfth year of his coronation, i.e., the sixteenth year of his reign. Now adding sixty-five (made up of sixteen years of Aśoka and forty-nine, the total of Chandragupta and Bindusāra) will bring us to 313 as the first regnal year of the former.

Roy makes short work of this argument by pointing out that all the Greek kings mentioned in Rock Edict XIII were living in 258 B.C. which is the date of the death of Magas of Cyrene, one of these kings. The edict therefore could not have been published later than 256 B.C. even when allowance is made of two years for the news of Magas's death to reach Pāṭaliputra. Then again Bactria is conspicuous by its absence in this Rock Edict. A powerful state, Bactria was on the confines of Aśoka's empire. How then is it that Aśoka did not think it necessary to establish cordial relations with it while he sent embassies to distant kingdoms of the Mediterranean? The answer is that Bactria did not exist. It became independent only in 256 B.C. The edict could not have been promulgated later than this date. Moreover, according to Ceylonese tradition, as seen above, Aśoka came to the throne 214 years after the Buddha. Subtracting 214 from 286, taking the latter year as the date of the Nirvāṇa, we get 272 as the date of Aśoka's accession. This would bring us to 256 B.C. as the twelfth year of Aśoka's coronation, the year in which the edict was promulgated.

Bhattasali had also sought support for his thesis from a *locus classicus* of Justin containing the following statement: "The author of the liberation was Sandrokottos... He having drawn together a band of robbers instigated the Indians to overthrow the existing government. When he was hereafter preparing to attack Alexander's prefects, an elephant of monstrous size approached him and received him on his back." Plutarch has also recorded, "Androcottos himself, who was but a youth, saw Alexander," the sum and substance of the deduction from these passages being that Androcottos became the king of Pāṭaliputra after driving away the Macedonian garrisons from the Punjab. But Eurdamos, one of the Macedonian prefects, was still lingering there. He did not leave India until 317. The liberation of the Punjab could not have been accomplished before that date. And if four years be accepted as the normal length of time required to complete the conquest of Magadha, there would be no incongruity in placing Chandragupta's accession in about 313 B.C.

However, as argued by Roy, Justin himself says that "having offended Alexander by his rashness, he (Chandragupta) saved himself by his swiftness of foot." This flight, according to Justin, occurred before Chandragupta gathered his army of mercenaries. It follows therefore that after his flight from Alexander's camp, Chandragupta collected a powerful army and with its help overthrew Alexander's prefects. And Roy triumphantly concludes that the existence of Eudamos in the North-West cannot preclude the possibility of Chandragupta's accession to the Indian throne about 324 B.C.

A Lost Historian

Roy's next contribution to Indian history was "Trogus' Source : A lost (?) Historian of the Hellenistic East," which he read at the third session of the Indian History Congress, Calcutta, 1939, and which appears in its *Proceedings*, pp. 328-47. In this paper Roy differs from Tarn who in his work *The Greeks in Bactria and India* claims to have brought to light what he terms, "Trogus' Source", meaning a lost author, the sole source Trogus Pompeius used for writing on Parthia and the Far East. This lost author, according to Tarn, knew much about India, had some knowledge of Jain and Buddhist literature and was acquainted with the *Mahābhārata*.

Roy's objection against Tarn's opinion that Trogus Pompeius drew his information about Parthia and the Far East from a sole source is that it is incredible that he left unutilised other sources available in his day. It is certain that Apollodorus (87 B.C.) was known in his times (20 B.C.-A.D. 9). One reason given by Tarn against the possibility of Trogus having drawn on Appollodorus is that Strabo (64 B.C.-A.D. 11) — who usually depends on Apollodorus—and Trogus have different accounts of the nomad conquest of Bactria. But the conflict between the two accounts is more apparent than real. For while Strabo enumerates the different ethnic groups responsible for that culmination, Trogus names the geographical regions whose inhabitants played a prominent part in the ruin of the Bactrian Greeks.

Tarn's claim for Trogus' Source's knowledge of Jaina literature is untenable, because the earliest Jaina works, *viz.* the canonical works were not put into writing before A.D. 454. And as for the Source's knowledge of Buddhism or Buddhist practices, it is farfetched to trace back the source of the story in the *Moralia* of Plutarch (who is indebted to Trogus' Source) of Menander's ashes being divided among the cities of his kingdom, each of which raised a *stupa* over its portion, to the Buddhist *Book of the Great Decease*. Even though this book also relates a similar story of the relics of the Buddha having been divided among eight peoples and enshrined under eight *stupas*, it need not have served as an incentive. True, Plutarch may have known Trogus' Source and utilized it. But Tarn misses the folklore element in the *Moralia* story. Fight over the corpse of the illustrious dead is a motif not of very rare occurrence in popular tales. Witness for instance the legend relating to the fight over the dead body of Kabir. But is one justified, asks Roy, in tracing all such tales to the Buddhist *Book of the Great Decease*? Then again, the word 'mneme' used by Plutarch for monuments is a general term signifying a building or a monument raised to the dead and has hardly any association with Buddhism.

As to the acquaintance of Trogus' Source with the *Mahābhārata*, the proof offered by Tarn is too tenuous to deserve serious consideration. It is as follows: Ptolemy, VII, 1.6, indebted to Trogus' Source, calls the country between the Indus and the Ravi 'Pandovuon or Pandaouon'. The same word appears in the form of Panda in the *Bessarica* of Dionysius. They are the Pāṇḍava-Pāṇḍu of the *Mahābhārata*. They do not appear in later history but belong solely to the epic. In consequence, Ptolemy and Dionysius got the name from some Greek who knew the *Mahābhārata*.

The fallacy of Tarn's argument, in the opinion of Roy, lies in the assumption that the Pāṇḍavas did not appear in history in the post-epic times and that the Pauravas occupying the region between the Jhelum and the Ravi were a different people. According to the epic the Pāṇḍavas were a branch of the Paurava family and were in control of the Chenab-Ravi region. They were in occupation of it in Alexander's time and they are represented in the Tibetan version of the *Vinaya Piṭaka*, *Mahāvagga*, VIII, i, as harassing King Pushkarasarin of Taxila, a contemporary of the Buddha.

It is creditable to Roy that Prof. Max Cary of the University of London should have sent the following appreciation to him on reading his article: "I am a great admirer of Tarn .... But I admit that sometimes his evidence goes too far, and I believe by your careful reasoning you have fairly caught him out on the question of Trogus' Source.... On the question of general method I quite agree with you that it is dangerous to assume that Trogus (or any other Greek or Roman writer) continuously drew upon a single source."

Arikamedu

It would appear from the bibliography of Roy's writings, meticulously prepared by Mr. T.K.G. Nair, his long-time admirer and friend, that the critique on Trogus' Source was followed by a study on the Nanda Dynasty. The paper was contributed to the fourth session of the Indian History Congress, 1940. It was, however, not published in its *Proceedings*. Nor is his paper "A Study on Encounter between Indian and Hellenistic Philosophy", contributed to the International Congress of Orientalists which met at New Delhi in 1964, published in the *Proceedings*. He also made a study of the Buddhist influences which substantially modified the spirit and technique of the Graeco-Roman and early Christian art in the Near East. An article on his findings was published in 1956 under the caption "Impact of Buddhism on Western Art." It is, however, not known where it was published. The same is the case with regard to a study he prepared on the archaeological site at Arikamedu, (Pondicherry), suggesting for it, in opposition to Sir R.E. Mortimer Wheeler, a pre-Christian dating and ascribing the settlement to Alexandrian traders. Submitted to Prof. Max Cary for opinion, the latter wrote to say : "I do not hesitate to accept your interpretation of the Arikamedu site as against Wheeler's. The stratification surely dates back in its earlier levels to the B.C. period."

Again in the fifties Roy contributed four important papers on Ancient India to the Societe Jean Bodin pour l' histoire comparative, Brussels. These papers were "Civic Administration in Ancient India," "Social and Economic problems of Urban India", "Private Law in Ancient Indian Cities", and "Indian Women in Antiquity". My best efforts have failed to trace the first two papers.

Indian Archaeology

The large amount of research that has been carried out in prehistoric, ancient and medieval India would not have been possible but for the signal service rendered over the years by the Archaeological Survey of India. And so it was fitting that, when the golden jubilee of the Survey as a Central Organisation came off in 1952, Roy should have been approached by the Department to write its history. His contribution appeared in the Special Jubilee Number of *Ancient India*, Vol. IX (1953), pp. 4-28 under the caption: 'Indian Archaeology from Jones to Marshall (1784-1902)". It was reproduced in book from with additional material under its new title *The Story of Indian Archaeology 1784-1947* (New Delhi, Archaeological Survey of India, 1961), 131 pp. + 48 pls.

Archaeological studies owe their beginning in India to the impetus given by Sir William Jones who along with an enthusiastic band of antiquarians founded the Asiatic Society on 15 January 1764 for the purpose of enquiring, among other things, "into the History, the Antiquities, Sciences and Literatures of Asia." These pioneers were ignorant of archaeological techniques, but versed as they were in literary researches, they confined themselves to translating and expounding ancient books and inscriptions. Foremost among them was Sir William Jones himself who by his epochal identification of Sandrokotos of the Greek historians with Chandragupta Maurya provided a sheet-anchor to Indian chronology. He also located the classical Palibotra at the confluence of the Ganga and the Son.

Against this "vertiable prince among scholars", Roy would not tolerate the least denigration. And so in his review of S.N. Mukherjee's *Sir William Jones*, a valiant defence of Jones lambasting a whole school of thought which sees in British rule only its negative side, he wrote : "Most far-reaching in their significance were the singular endeavours Jones made to lift the veil of obscurity from the face of India's past.... Add to all these that he was a poet whose impassioned outpourings had a deep impact on a whole generation of English men of letters ranging from Southey and Moore to Shelley; a man of action always ready to throw his weight on the side of the depressed and the down-trodden; and finally a humanist whose intense warmth had an invigorating influence on whomsoever he happened to encounter; and you will at once realise why Samuel Johnson felt prompted to hail him as the most enlightened among the sons of men." (*Indian Economic and Social History Review*, Vol. VIII (1971), pp. 321-27 hereinafter *IESHR*).

Archaeology took a giant stride with the appointment of James Prinsep as the Secretary of the Asiatic Society. He assumed direction of the entire archaeological work in India. Among his major achievements was the decipherment of the Brahmi and the Kharoshthi scripts and the unravelling of the secrets of the inscriptions of Piyadasi, leading to the identification of the latter with Aśoka and the establishment of his contemporaneity with Antiochus III and Ptolemy Philadelphos. This helped to base Indian chronology on a secure foundation.

Meanwhile, the Royal Asiatic Society of Great Britain and Ireland had begun to evince interest in the preservation of the historical monuments in India. But it was only after the troublesome times of the 'Mutiny' were over that the Government could settle down to discharge its cultural responsibilities. It passed an Act (X) in 1861 thereby assuming the duty "to prevent injury to, and preserve, buildings remarkable for their antiquity or for their historical or architectural value." Roy rightly observes "that this departure from the old policy of apathy and downright neglect may be appropriately regarded as marking the birth of a new conscience in the country."

Although Cunningham was appointed Archaeological Surveyor soon after the passing of this Act, it was only in 1870 that the Archaeological Survey of India was established, and it was in February 1871 that he took charge of the office of Director General.

He immediately applied himself to a survey of the country. He deserves the meed of praise for his pioneering work, the twenty-three volumes of his survey reports constituting a rich mine of information.

He had, however, no aptitude for prehistory, though he was, as Roy picturesquely puts it, "within an ace of an epoch-making discovery in 1873, when he unearthed at Harappa a pictographic seal along with many specimens of Harappan pottery. But he scarcely understood that they were the fragments of a great past civilisation. He touched it, but passed it by."

The next Director, James Burgess, assumed the post on 25 March 1886. He at once proceeded to supply a want which had been left unfulfilled in northern surveys so far: to provide a full illustration and history of ancient and medieval architecture. To this end he had careful architectural surveys carried out either under his own direction or by his colleagues. Most noteworthy of these activities was the elaborate survey made by Fuhrer and Smith between 1886 and 1887 of the Sharqui architecture of Jaunpur and of the monuments of Zafarabad, Saheth Maheth and Ayodhya, the operations carried out by Smith during 1888-89 in Badaon, Lalitpur, Orchha and other places in Bundelkhand, the survey of ancient architecture in North Gujarat and the Muslim architecture at Bijapur by Henry Cousens, and that of the monuments at Mahabalipuram and the remains in Krishna, Nellore and Godavari Districts completed by Rea during the same period.

Another lasting service of Burgess was a quarterly publication *Epigraphia Indica* which he started in October 1888. He was able to bring out in two years as many as eight fascicules of this publication, containing highly valuable inscriptions edited by renowned epigraphists, Buhler, Kielhorn and Eggeling. Earlier,

Burgess himself had compiled a volume of Sanskrit and Tamil inscriptions, and his colleague, Hultzsch, collected and edited a huge corpus of inscriptions enough to fill three large volumes. The publication of the results of his survey went on uninterrupted, and during his fifteen years' service, he was able to bring out no less than twenty magnificent volumes. Of these seven formed part of the *Archaeological Survey of India, New Imperial Series*.

John Marshall

Indian archaeology had been brought almost to the verge of dissolution what with the unimaginative proposals of Burgess readily accepted by the Government. On his assumption of the viceregal office Curzon was amazed to find, on a study of the system in each province, that it was "impossible to conceive a system more chaotic or futile in practice." He recorded in a Minute of 23 September 1899 : "No Local Government is, per se, interested in archaeology.... Thus, it has come about that, owing to the absence of any central and duly qualified authority, not merely are beautiful and famous buildings crumbling to decay; but there is neither principle nor unity in conservation or repair, while from time to time horrors are committed that make the student shudder and turn grey."

The result was that in the definite proposals made to the Secretary of State on 20 December 1900 the Government of India recommended the revival of the post of Director General axed at the suggestion of Burgess. The incumbent of this office was to be a trained explorer combining archaeological knowledge with engineering skill. He would be required to exercise general supervision over the entire archaeological work in the country, co-ordinating and bringing up to date the local surveys and reports and in addition present to Government an annual report of his own work.

The proposals were sanctioned by the Secretary of State on 29 November 1901—experimentally for a five-year term, and Sir John Marshall, who had already worked in Greece, South Turkey and Crete, was selected for the post on the recommendation of the British Museum.

Marshall who remained in command of the archaeological field for over a quarter of a century and saw the Survey grow into a massive, gigantic structure had to start literally from scratch. Before his time, archaeology had meant simply a quest for *objects d'art* or religious relics. Marshall was resolved to make it serve a purpose altogether different. To borrow the words of Roy : "He wanted it, first and foremost, to recapture the total culture of India in past ages with their cities and streets, their furniture and tools, their arms and weapons, their ornaments and jewels, their seals and coins and their laws and customs. To this one end was keyed most of his exploration programme, as would be amply evidenced by the number and historical importance of the ancient sites laid bare during his regime—Nalanda and Vaisali, Pataliputra and Bhita, three cities of Taxila, and, crowning all, the proto-historic towns of Mohenjo-daro and Harappa. Not only did he conceive these and other programmes, but with his master hand he worked out all the details, fixed and wrote down the methods, and sketched also the blue-prints for all future research."

Marshall also dispatched exploratory missions to India's border-lands to obtain material for reconstructing his history of India's contacts with Central Asia, Tibet and China. Sir Aurel Stein led three expeditions for this purpose in 1900, 1906-1908 and 1913-16. Stein described his discoveries in the eleven quarto volumes of his *Ancient Khotan* (1907), *Serindia* (1921) and *Innermost Asia* (1928).

These were amazing achievements. But more astounding were the discoveries of R.D. Banerji at Mohenjo-daro in Sind yielding seals akin to the ones discovered at Harappa by Cunningham fifty years earlier and by Daya Ram Sahni more recently. The announcement of these discoveries by Marshall in the *Illustrated London News* (20 September 1924) took the world of archaelogoists literally by storm. Prof. Sayce pointed out the resemblance between the antiquities from Indus Valley and certain Sumerian objects, and Gadd and Sydney Smith traced the affinities between Indian and Babylonian relics. Marshall described the results of the excavations of 1921-27 in three monumental volumes, *Mohenjo-daro and the Indus Civilisation* (London 1931).

As Roy has so aptly put it: "Marshall will always be remembered as the man who, archaeologically speaking, left India three thousand years older than he had found her."

Mortimer Wheeler

The appointment of Mortimer Wheeler, an eminent British archaeologist, as Director General ushered in a new era.

His first task was that of re-studying Indus cities with a view to determining their sociological character. His discovery of the flood-worn remains of a citadel exploded the prevailing myth of the non-military character of the Indus cities. To establish inter-relationship between India and the West with the aid of the Roman coins and other material that would surface while digging, he selected for the purpose Arikamedu. We have already referred to the interpretation by Roy of that material. Another service of Wheeler was the transformation of "the entire character of the excavation methods followed in India by subordinating them to stratigraphical control and analysis conformably to the best international standard."

His tenure of office as Director General is one of the most eventful in the annals of Indian archaeology.

Roy had pressed so much material into the production of the book and estimated with critical acumen the services of each and every scholar who had anything to do with Indian archaeology that the book evoked the following tribute from Professor Tucci : "I have perused your book with great interest admiring your achievement in collecting such a mass of material in so small a compass."

Modern India

Knowing as he did the National Archives as the palm of his hand, Roy possessed first-hand knowledge of British India. He compiled an entirely new study of the Black Hole episode on the basis of hitherto unpublished and unknown material, collected by him from the Fort St. George archives, India Office and the Dutch archives. This study was awaiting publication. He wrote a biographical study of the Rani of Jhansi on the basis of her own correspondence in Marathi and in English translations as well as other contemporary records. He prepared a disquisition on the Gandhi-Irvin Pact on the basis of new material available among the late Home Department records; and his work on Nain Singh, the famous explorer responsible for placing Tibet and greater part of Asia on the map, was nearing completion. Mr. T.K.G. Nair, however, searched for these works in vain. I also regret I have not been able to obtain a copy of his paper "A Critique of the Sources of the Economic History of India during the Eighteenth and the Nineteenth Century," contributed by him to the Economic History Conference held under the auspices of the Delhi School of Economics in 1962. He has presented in this paper an assessment of the value of the *Survey of India's memoirs* as a first hand source of economic history. Roy's collaboration with Verrier Elwin, the noted anthropologist, is acknowledged by the latter in his books *The Bondo Highlander*, *Myths of Mid India*, and *Religion of an Indian Tribe*.

Among his published papers "The Surat Firman", contributed to the *Prof. C.S. Srinivasachari Sixth-first Birthday Celebration Volume* (Madras, 1950), pp. 225-31 is of interest because the Imperial Mughal Grant, of which Roy speaks, constitutes the first recognition by the strongest military power in India of the British naval supremacy in the Indian seas. As the British empire in India was essentially the creation of the British sea power, the document may be regarded as marking the beginning of that empire. It is however curious that none of the writers who have referred to the document has a clear notion about either its date or the circumstances leading to its issue. Roy attempts to ascertain these circumstances with the help of the documents of the period. The documents show that on 10 October 1612 the terms of the treaty presented by Captain Best on behalf of the Company were agreed to by the Governor of Ahmedabad after three days' conference. These terms laid down the conditions for English trade in the cities of Surat, Ahmedabad, Goga or in any other part or parts of the country within the Great Mughal's dominions. The confirmation of the articles, however, did not arrive within the stipulated time. In the meanwhile, the Portuguese sent four galleons to dispute the passage of the English ships. But in the naval encounter that ensued the English ships put the Portuguese squardorn to flight. The success of the English pleased the Mughals. The farman was received by the English on 20 February 1613.

Our Loss

Highly gifted as he was, Roy would have made a mark in any avocation suitable to his abilities. His teachers were so impressed by him that Professor S.C. Sen Gupta, his professor of English who later became the Principal of the Presidency College, Calcutta, was only voicing the opinion of his colleagues when he wrote that Roy was the best pupil he had taught and one of the most cultured men he had met. The marvel of such a man, however, does not rest on what he was capable of doing. For talents of mind and music are simply gifts received from God and need not form a source of special tribute. Rather we should look to what a recipient of such gifts has done with them. It would be agreed from the study we have made of his writings that Roy emerges as an outstanding archivist and brilliant historian. He carried out to the extent he was capable what he conceived to be the task of the Indian historian: to unravel the structure and the development of the Indian society as a whole. He insisted that the historian's primary duty is to give the facts and that history should be non-partisan, and himself practised the precept. He held that historical research is strictly conditioned by the availability of the sources of the necessary type and quality. He helped in making this possible by inspiring and assisting the publication programme of the National Archives of India. And for the rest, he hoped that the historian of modern India would make full use of the archival sources taking advantage of the opening of the National and State Archives to the public. "He himself did much," as Professor Holden Furber has aptly remarked in his splendid tribute to him, "to make possible the work of many scholar Indian and foreign, who have illumined India's modern history."